LONGMAN GROUP UK LIMITED
*Longman House, Burnt Mill, Harlow, Essex CM20 2JE, UK
and Associated Companies throughout the World.*

Published in the United States of America
by Longman Inc., New York.

*First published 1986
ISBN 0 582 35528 1*

Set in 10/11pt Bembo, Linotron 202

*Printed in Great Britain
by William Clowes (Beccles) Ltd.*

British Library Cataloguing in Publication Data

Dutton, Brian
The media. — (Sociology in focus series)
1. Mass media — Social aspects
I. Title   II. Series
302.2'34   HM258

ISBN 0-582-35528-1

Library of Congress Cataloguing in Publicaton Data

Dutton, Brian.
  The media.

  (Sociology in focus series)
  Bibliography: p.
  Includes index.
  Summary: A discussion of media, their production and audience, with the
intention of integrating the topic into a study of sociology.
  1. Mass media. [1. Mass media] I. Title. II. Series.
P90.D946Me 1986   302.2'34   86-101
ISBN 0-582-35528-1

Contents

Acknowledgements

We are grateful to the following for permission to reproduce copyright material:

Associated Book Publishers (UK) Ltd for an extract from pp 76–79 *Understanding News* by J Hartley (Methuen & Co 1982); Association for Education in Journalism and Mass Communication for an adapted extract from the article 'Platforms and Windows: Broadcasting's role in election campaigns' in *Journalism Quarterly* Summer 1971 Copyright 1971; the author's agent for adapted extracts from pp 31, 38–40 *Folk Devils and Moral Panics* by S Cohen (MacGibbon & Kee Ltd 1972); the author, Professor S Hall for an extract from his article 'Mugging; a case study of the media' pp 571–572 *The Listener* (1/5/75); The Open University for an adapted extract from pp 20–22 *Science, Technology and Popular Culture* (1) (1982) Copyright 1982 The Open University Press; Pluto Press for an adapted extract from pp 30–31 *On Television* by S Hood (Pluto Press 1980).

I would like to thank Barbara Johnstone for typing the manuscript.

To Susan

Series introduction

Sociology in Focus aims to provide an up-to-date, coherent coverage of the main topics that arise on an introductory course in sociology. While the intention is to do justice to the intricacy and complexity of current issues in sociology, the style of writing has deliberately been kept simple. This is to ensure that the student coming to these ideas for the first time need not become lost in what can appear initially as jargon.

Each book in the series is designed to show something of the purpose of sociology and the craft of the sociologist. Throughout the different topic areas the interplay of theory, methodology and social policy have been highlighted, so that rather than sociology appearing as an unwieldy collection of facts, the student will be able to grasp something of the process whereby sociological understanding is developed. The format of the books is broadly the same throughout. Part one provides an overview of the topic as a whole. In part two the relevant research is set in the context of the theoretical, methodological and policy issues. The student is encouraged to make his or her own assessment of the various arguments, drawing on the statistical and reference material provided both here and at the end of the book. The final part of the book contains both statistical material and a number of 'Readings'. Questions have been provided in this section to direct students to analyse the materials presented in terms of both theoretical assumptions and methodological approaches. It is intended that this format should enable students to exercise their own sociological imaginations rather than to see sociology as a collection of universally accepted facts, which just have to be learned.

While each book in the series is complete within itself, the similarity of format ensures that the series as a whole provides an integrated and balanced introduction to sociology. It is intended that the text can be used both for individual and classroom study, while the inclusion of the variety of statistical and documentary materials lend themselves to both the preparation of essays and brief seminars.

It is dangerous to let the public behind the scenes. They are easily disillusioned and then they are angry with you, for it was the illusion they loved.

W. Somerset Maugham, *The Summing Up*, Heinemann, 1952.

PART 1

Introduction

---

1 Perspectives on the media

'The media' is a term which forms part of the vocabulary of everyday conversation, a reference to the institutions of communication which comprise of various forms of sound, vision and print, but principally television, radio and the press. We, the viewers, listeners and readers, are willing to spend literally years of our lives consuming the products of the media, as the statistics for British audiences testify (see Fig. 6.1 in Part 3).

Doubtless you, the reader, will be reflecting on how closely you resemble the average media consumer, but you are unlikely to be one of the 3 per cent of households without a television set (indeed you are more than likely to have two sets) or 20 per cent of households not purchasing a newspaper. Thus the media does truly reach a 'mass' audience in a way which few can ignore, so it is not surprising to find that sociologists are only one group in a long list of interested parties who speculate on the role of the media in contemporary society. Politicians, trade union leaders, church leaders, royalty, teachers and judges are but a few who regularly voice opinions about the media and most are critical of its effects (whilst not hesitating to use it to channel their protests).

To quote James Halloran (1970),

> Television has been criticized for producing conformity, for operating in the interests of political and economic vested interest, for maintaining the status quo, diminishing the power and habit of critical thinking, concentrating on the trivial and on the sensational, standing in the way of a truly participatory democracy, producing a deterioration in aesthe-

tic taste and general cultural standards and for nullifying hard won social gains, particularly in education . . .

The role of the media in society is the subject of this book. Whilst it is recognised that TV, films, newspapers, etc., are popular forms of communication, the exact nature of their social significance is much disputed. In this section, I will briefly outline the main theoretical perspectives which have contributed to the sociological debate about the media.

Traditional *functionalist* sociologists have not been prominent in the debate, but have tended to view the media as having an integrative role, maintaining consensus through reinforcing central values in a way which is beneficial to society. In particular, American functionalists, such as Daniel Bell, have stressed the importance of the media in helping shape western societies as mass democracies in which all can participate and be informed.

A closely related perspective is that of *pluralism*, which derives principally from an analysis of the distribution of power in society. It shares with functionalism a belief that the media aids democracy and meets the needs and interests of its consumers, whilst recognising that industrial society is not comprised of a unity or consensus, but rather has many competing interest groups struggling to gain their ends. This diversity of opinion is reflected in the wide range of media products available on the market. For example, in Britain the communist paper the *Morning Star* sharply contrasts politically with conservative papers like the *Daily Telegraph* or the *Daily Mail*, or in women's magazines there is the contrast between the feminist *Spare Rib* and the 'traditional' *Woman's Own* or *The Lady*. Supply meets demand in the free market, is the essence of the pluralist theory of the media.

The *uses and gratifications* theory fits the functionalist tradition at an individual level. This focuses on the ways in which the media meets various individual needs, be they psychological or social. This represents an advance on the more simplistic notion of the media, especially cinema, providing 'escapist' pleasures (simplistic because 'escapism' can cover a variety of differing pleasures, and besides, is it possible to contrast the real world with the 'unreal' of the media?).

Far more critical is the view offered by the *conflict* perspective and its roots firmly in Marxist theory. Here the media is seen as a device for *social control* by the dominant or ruling groups in society, be they a capitalist class, patriarchy, white racial group or any other such ruling group. The media supports the interests of such groups by presenting the world in an *ideological* way, i.e. presenting only a partial picture of reality, and, in so doing, helping to prevent opposition arising. In contast to the pluralist version, the individual consumer is not seen as sovereign. Media supply is tightly controlled by large corporations, since there is a concentration of ownership of media outlets in a market in which entry is made extremely difficult by large capital costs and legal restrictions.

Rather than concentrating on the media as part of the social structure, i.e. as an institution related to other social institutions like government and education, the *interactionist* theory is concerned with the subjective view of both media producers and consumers, and how they define and interpret the world. No assumptions are made about the role of the media in society, but rather emphasis is placed on the different meanings given to its products by media professionals or viewers and readers. In this way, the interactionist contribution may be complementary to the other perspectives rather than in direct opposition. For example, the interactionist might study the way a journalist selects and presents a story, what views of the social world s/he holds, how the role of journalist is defined, etc. A Marxist (structural) perspective would primarily involve trying to see how far those views may be shaped by wider social and economic forces, e.g. the need to produce a profitable newspaper, or the requirement to stay within the law. This is a matter of emphasis. Much of the research into the media involves a blend of theories (e.g. Marxism and interactionism), or is not explicitly representative of a particular theory.

The areas of debate

One of the problems in discussing the sociological debate about the media is that there is no agreement as to what it is specifically about the media that is being analysed. This follows logically from the competing theortical perspectives mentioned above in that each theory carries different assumptions about the media's role in society, i.e. about its relationship to other institutions, to different social groups, etc., and these assumptions have tended to direct the individual sociologists, be they Marxist, pluralist, etc., to concentrate on one particular aspect of the media whilst ignoring others. Just as in other areas of sociology, it is very difficult, if not impossible, to be neutral and open-minded prior to investigating or theorising about the media.

It also follows that the different perspectives have not used the same methods of studying the media, and therefore often use very different kinds of evidence to support their theory. For example, whilst the uses and gratifications theory has focused on the active individual consumer obtaining certain needs from watching television, Marxists have focused on both the economic forces affecting the media and the cultural meaning of media products.

The three distinctive aspects of the media which have come under scrutiny are production, representations and audience.

1 Production

There is a popular view that it is the technology of the media, the means by which messages pass from their source to the audience, which is the all-powerful force at work. This is reflected in Marshall McLuhan's maxim that 'the medium is the message'. Few, if any, sociologists adopt this line of thought, since to do so is to ignore the complex social, economic and political processes which help shape the media production. For example, Britons travelling to America are usually bewildered by the diet of programmes that American television has to offer, whilst Americans visiting Britain are equally perplexed at the content of the popular tabloid newspapers on sale over here.

For Marxists, ownership of the means of production is ultimately the determining factor in the analysis of any social practice. In this case, ownership of the media is seen as a key element in the mental domination of the capitalist class over the rest of society. Rather than a free market where each group's interests are supplied by a wide variety of media outlets, Marxists argue that, just as in the business world in general, there is an ever-decreasing number of owners and a tightening grip of the market by the large multinational corporations.

Within the debate about whether there is still a ruling class in industrial societies, the ownership versus control of business argument is prominent. Do not the managers, who have no shares in companies but are merely employees, really control modern industry with their professional expertise and skill? The same question is raised about the media professionals who 'manage' and 'control' television and newspaper production. Those favouring an interactionist approach have looked at professionals working in media organisations (not forgetting that in Britain the BBC does not answer to any shareholders but is publicly owned), and suggested that professional autonomy may exist in large business corporations in a way which suggests that the Marxist view is unduly deterministic.

Another line of attack is from the pluralists who cite the persistence of smaller independent media outlets to cater for interests which might be seen as anti-capitalist, such as left wing journals or critical television series (the controversy over some early Channel 4 programmes aimed at 'minority groups' is a typical example). Those readers who follow the pop/rock business will be aware of the success of independent record labels which periodically capture the market with new developments in the music before usually being taken over the larger established labels. These issues are discussed in Chapter 2, but to some extent their resolution depends upon an examination of media products.

2 Representations

Analysis of media representations has occupied a wide range of sociologists (not to mention psychologists, linguists and other academics) in recent years, but the central ground has been occupied by the Marxist perspective. The interests of the ruling group (be it a ruling class, patriarchy, etc.) are maintained through the media reproducing a dominant ideology, a set of beliefs and ideas which represent those interests as natural.

It is relatively simple to demonstrate ideological bias in the popular press, but isn't television news neutral and impartial? Not so according to many sociologists who have tried to expose the falsity of that claim, and instead shown it to be a social construction, reflecting the values of news journalists who inevitably if unwittingly either share the attitudes and values of those in power, or give the powerful privileged access to define the issues in their terms. A prominent example of research into this area is the work done by the Glasgow Media Group, who have painstakingly conducted a content analysis of hundreds of news broadcasts, focusing on the coverage of key economic and political issues, especially industrial relations.

The power to define the world, set the agenda and give meaning to events and actions is something which was highlighted much earlier by those sociologists working on the labelling theory (i.e. interactionist) of deviance. The media has been identified as a major source of labels which have stigmatised various groups and placed them outside an assumed consensus of what is socially normal and acceptable. Stan Cohen's study of the press coverage of the mods and rockers skirmishes in British seaside resorts in the mid 1960s is a notable example of the effects of media labelling, transforming groups of teenagers into 'folk devils', and helping to create a 'moral panic' about the threat to social order by 'deviant' youth groups. In this way, Cohen and others have attempted to show that definitions of morality, normality, etc., are not absolute or constant, but subject to negotiation, dependent on who is doing the defining, and more importantly who has the power to define, interpret or label social groups or situations as acceptable, deviant or otherwise.

From the interactionist perspective, language cannot be neutral, and so media communication, be it in words or images, requires interpretation. Those sociologists working within a Marxist theory have tried to show how media language reflects the interests of those groups with most power in society. Marxists have made the running, but the ideologies of patriarchy, racism, and even ageism (e.g. the failure to show elderly people as other than dependent, weak, victims, etc.) have also been detected in media representations. How the media defines social reality is taken up in Chapter 3.

3 Audience

The sociologist analysing media representations can happily replay videos of television programmes, scrutinise newspaper and magazine columns in an attempt to read or decode cultural meanings. However, much more problematic is the audiences' reading of media messages. In debating where power lies in society, pluralists are critical of the Marxists' preoccupation with concentration of wealth, connections between politicians and business corporations, etc., whilst ignoring the actual outcome of decision-making processes. Similarly, they argue that no assumptions can be made about the effects that the media have upon the audience without a rigorous empirical investigation of such effects. Furthermore, pluralists claim that research into audience effects has shown that the audience is pluralistic, i.e. composed of many different social groups, and has many different orientations towards the media. This fact above all, they claim, shapes the media's content. In other words, the media supplies a diversity of products to meet a diversified audience's needs.

Others have attempted to isolate the specific individual needs, or uses and gratifications, which audience members actively seek from the media. This has an element of psychological functionalism in that the media's purpose or function appears to be fulfilling various audience 'needs'. In addition, there is the interactionist perspective of the audience as active interpreters of what they select to consume, usually in relation to 'significant others' – relatives, friends, colleagues, etc.

'To get away from the habit of thinking in terms of what media does to people, and substitute for it the idea of what people do with the media' has been one result of singling out the audience as the key variable in the sociology of the media. Even those who feel that ownership and content are important variables have had to take into account the interrelationship between ideological forms of media representations and a variety of 'meaning systems' carried by the audience according to their social location. This is to recognise that it may be possible for the audience to produce a radically different reading of a media product than was intended by its producers. Thus, for example, regular viewers of *Dallas* may enjoy it for its unsympathetic, and hence critical, portrayal of American business and bourgeois family life instead of the more usual gratifications of diversion, escapism, etc. Sociological and psychological perspectives of the audience are the theme of Chapter 4.

It is obvious from the above that the sociology of the media is multidimensional – that there are several aspects of the media to investigate, and that no one perspective is guaranteed to provide the truth. As always in sociology, theoretical values and methodological preferences are at work. In the last section of this introduction, I would like to sketch an outline of how the debate has evolved historically, and by doing so hopefully put the theoretical debate into a clearer perspective. It might also be apparent that the way in which the media debate has unfolded reflects the changing shifts of sociological fashion during the last fifty years.

How the debate has evolved

Phase 1: mass society 1900–30s

Mass society theory flourished in the 1930s as part of a general theory of social change which followed on from Tönnies' distinction between *gemeinschaft* and *gesellschaft*. The belief that the new urban areas were populated by a 'mass' of isolated individuals, rootless, alienated and deprived of face to face primary group social relations typical of the rural village, led many writers to speculate that such individuals were extremely vulnerable to the emergent forms of impersonal mass communication: the cinema and the radio. These fears were reinforced by the rise of the Nazi party in Germany, which appeared to be able to mobilise popular support through its effective use of the mass media as vehicles for its political propaganda. Thus the mass media was capable of mass manipulation.

Although relying almost entirely on unsupported speculation, this model of a powerful force exploiting an ignorant mass (sometimes known as the 'hypodermic needle' theory) has maintained a popular appeal among a variety of social and political commentators. We have been alerted to the dangers of insidious mass advertising preying on our unconscious, of the popular media creating illiteracy and debasing cultural standards, of violence on our screens producing a nation of callous juvenile hooligans, and numerous other 'moral panics' within the framework of a mass manipulative model of the media. Television, in particular, has been singled out as all-powerful – TV controllers being referred to as the 'new priesthood' (with the decline of the church's influence in society), and the world seen as reduced to a 'global village' via the means of the TV screen. Within sociological circles, however, support for the mass society theory declined after the war due to a growing body of evidence which contradicted the theory's claims.

Phase 2: effects studies 1940s–60s

Once empirical research into measuring the actual effects which the media had on its audience was undertaken, it quickly became apparent that the audience was far from being a mass of isolated individuals, but instead members of distinctive social groups. Within such groups 'opinion leaders' would interpret media messages on behalf of the rest of the group in a process which became known as the 'two step flow' (see p. 51).

Also, social psychological research of media consumption showed that the audience both selected and filtered from what was available, rejecting messages which were not consonant with existing attitudes or beliefs, so that in the long run the media were simply reinforcing these attitudes and beliefs, not changing them. This helped to explain, it was argued, the impotence of the media to make any impact on political opinions of the voters during election campaigns.

The uses and gratifications model of the media was a natural development from this effects research, focusing on what individual needs were supplied or gratified by a media industry anxious to maximise its audience rather than change them in any way. This shift towards a view of the media as largely in harmony with its audience is to some degree a reflection of the period in question. Functionalist accounts of consensus and social integration were dominant, and the western nations (especially USA) were experiencing unprecedented prosperity.

Phase 3: the media as ideology 1960s onwards

During the late 1960s, a series of social and political upheavals disrupted the prevailing stability and 'consensus'. Race riots in American cities, striking workers in western Europe and protesting anti-war students on both sides of the Atlantic helped to create a more critical academic atmosphere, not least in Marxist theory. As such, the media soon came under scrutiny, and the conventional wisdom was challenged. The results and conclusions of effects studies were criticised on the grounds that the wrong questions were being asked about the media and its potential social influence. Could political effects simply be measured by looking at voting preferences and media use in an election campaign? What about the long term cumulative political effects of daily news and current affairs coverage?

Of course, such long term effects could never be empirically measured by interviewing audiences 'before' and 'after'. The whole process was too subtle and long term, and besides, both the media and audience could not be isolated for research purposes from their social context, as some psychologists still attempt to do with television. Seen as a cultural product, and part of a broader concern with the sociology of knowledge, media researchers began to look at media representations in terms of their ideological content, thus raising questions of power. The media has come to be recognised as a crucial *cultural institution* in which ideas and meanings are created and circulated within society.

The 1970s saw a huge growth in media research, which began in the developing centres of mass communications and media studies university departments, and has since spread across into the emergent fields of cultural and linguistic studies in a cross fertilisation of approaches. This has produced a wealth of material covering everything from the analysis of *Coronation Street* and *The Sweeney* to James Bond and women's magazines, and shows no sign of slowing down in the 1980s.

PART 2

The main aspects of the media

2 Production

Cultural production

Television, films, records, etc., are all examples of cultural production. Unlike, say, a television set or record player, which are primarily material goods bought for a specific use, cultural products contain social meanings, ideas, knowledge, taste, etc. Whether that makes cultural products really any different from material products is open to question. It is possible to look at *Gone with the Wind* as simply a film which has been sold worldwide, as something to be consumed in the same way as food or clothing or as a meaningful film which says a lot about American history in the deep south. To take a second example, we might consider the song 'White Christmas'. On the one hand, the composer, Irving Berlin, may have been expressing a personal and emotional sentiment. On the other hand, his song may have been written to meet the requirements of the record company to which he was contracted, who could then market the song and make it one of the best selling, and hence profitable, songs of all time.

To pursue this issue further, two interrelated aspects of the media have to be investigated in depth, namely its economic organisation and the contribution of those who work within the media and are responsible for its production. Many sociologists have described the media as an *industry*, producing cultural goods for mass consumption with one overriding motive: profit. In fact the term 'culture industry' was used in the 1940s by members of the *Frankfurt School* of critical theory (a Marxist-influenced group) to refer to cultural products being mass produced in a manner no different from motor cars: 'for automobiles, there are such differences as the number of cylinders, cubic capacity, details of patented gadgets; for films there are the number of stars, the extravagant use of technology, labour and equipment, and the introduction of the latest psychological formulas' (Adorno and Horkheimer, in Curran *et al.*, 1977).

Others have concentrated on the media as an *institution*, comprising an organisational structure with established practices and norms within which media professionals work with some degree of freedom from the external demands of the owners to make profitable cultural products. The extent to which the media resembles an industry such as motor car manufacturing can best be approached through the key issue of who owns and controls the media.

Ownership versus control: Marx

In a much quoted passage in *The German Ideology*, Marx wrote that 'The class which has the means of material production at its disposal has control at the same time over the production and distribution of the ideas of their age.' Very simply, the ruling class, the owners of the means of production, also own, and therefore control, the means of cultural production, including the media, which enables their ideas to become the ruling ideas of the day.

Exactly how this control over cultural production is exercised has been the subject of considerable sociological debate. A very crude Marxist might emphasise direct intervention by capitalist media owners in the manner of, say, a press baron like Rupert Murdoch, who has been known personally to dictate the editorial policies of the newspapers he owns (in Britain these include *The Times* and the *Sun*). Marx was able to gain first hand information of the lack of freedom of journalists through his experience of working for the *New York Daily Tribune* (now owned by Rupert Murdoch). He argued that the determining constraint was always the economic pressure produced under capitalism, regardless of any direct interference by the owners of the media. It is this point which subsequent Marxist writers have held to be as important today as when Marx was alive.

The latter part of the nineteenth century witnessed a change in the nature of capital ownership. In order to raise capital for expansion, companies began to sell shares to outsiders, thus becoming what is now known as joint stock companies, or corporations. The owners of companies then tended to be shareholders, who left the responsibility of running the business to the managers, who themselves might not actually share in the ownership of the firms. Marx did not see that this made any difference to the class structure, as real control still lay with the owners, whose interests were served by the employed managers.

A critique of Marx: the managerial revolution

Marx's theory came under increasing attack in the 1930s and 1940s from those writers who argued that a real shift in power base had occurred with the growth of large scale organisations. The shareholders, the 'owners', no longer exercised real power. This lay with a new group or 'class': the managers. In 1932, Berle and Means (1968) claimed that 65 per cent of America's top 200 non-banking corporations were management controlled. Corporations were classed as under management control if the largest shareholding group held less than a fifth of the total shares. By this they meant that managers were able to govern company policy, since shareholders were a diverse group, unorganised and relatively ignorant, and thus unable to challenge the expertise and cohesion of the management.

Perhaps the best known contribution to this argument was **James Burnham**, whose book *The Managerial Revolution* (first published in 1941) helped to popularise the concept. He foresaw the rise of managerial power at both company and state level in capitalist America and communist Russia. This idea has evolved into the notion of 'corporate state', in which a plurality of groups, but especially the managerial elite, combine to administer and control the modern state, representing a rejection of Marx's idea of the capitalist state controlled by the owners of the means of production.

This debate has significant implications for questions of where power lies in society, the managerial elite thesis challenging the Marxist ruling class theory, and suggesting that power may be more diffuse in the modern industrial state. With regard to the media, it shifts the emphasis away from the issue of who owns the media, or has overall *allocative* control, to one of who actually is concerned with the daily running of media organisations, those with *operational* control. Is it not the case that those with the expertise and knowledge to run a modern media organisation, i.e. the media professionals, are largely autonomous (self-governing)? This point seems particularly strong when the example of the BBC is noted. The BBC is a central media institution, publicly owned, and bound by a legal prescription to operate a policy of impartiality, in much the way that pluralists view the role of the modern state, a neutral institution of government, reflecting the wide diversity of interests in a modern industrial society.

The Marxist reply: (1) concentration of ownership

Marx predicted that successful capitalist enterprises would grow in size until a few companies would dominate the market. This trend has been identified by modern Marxist writers, including those charting the progress of a small number of large corporations who now have a high degree of concentrated ownership in the media industry.

Murdock and Golding (1977) are critical of the managerialist theory on two main grounds.

1 By just looking at the relationships between owners and managers within individual companies they ignore the *interconnections between shareholders* of different companies, and thus underestimate the potential power base of owner control.
2 Whatever freedom the managers may appear to have in pursuing their own ends, they are still constrained by one fundamental need, *the maximisation of profits*. No shareholder will tolerate management inefficiency in this respect.

In great empirical detail, Murdock and Golding outline the shift towards concentration of ownership in the various media sectors through the process of mergers and takeovers, so that by the beginning of the 1970s the top five firms in the respective sectors accounted for:

71 per cent daily newspaper circulation
74 per cent homes with commercial television
78 per cent admissions to cinemas
70 per cent paperback sales
65 per cent record sales

They argue that this trend has led to a reduction in competition between companies and that we have therefore now entered a phase of monopoly capitalism where small companies are being gradually squeezed out and potential new entrants lack the resources to be able effectively to compete with the giants. For example, in the press, the only national daily or Sunday newspapers to be launched in Britain in recent years, the *Daily Star* and the *Mail on Sunday*, emanated from existing companies wanting to use spare press capacity.

What Murdock and Golding consider to be even more significant has been the ever-increasing interconnections between sectors of the media industry, i.e. the large corporations have acquired interests in several media forms. This process of *diversification* and branching out has led to the formation of huge *conglomerates*. This is part of a general tendency for the leading firms in the economy to acquire a greater proportion of the overall means of production, so that by 1969, the top 100 companies in Britain controlled nearly two-thirds of British industry. The aim of these conglomerates is to spread their risks through a variety of industries in order to protect their profits, which might be squeezed by staying in one sector alone.

Media imperialism

The conglomerates referred to above have expanded their influence outside the western industrialised countries like Britain into the newly developing countries of the Third World. These countries often do not have the economic and technological resources with which to set up their own media industry, and so have accepted what has been provided by large American and European corporations. Marxists have seen this as a new kind of capitalist empire building, a form of economic and cultural imperialism (see Fig. 2.1).

The media as industry

Industrial production, with visions of mass manufacture of standardised goods in factory conditions, which are then sold in the market place to the public, seems a long way from the popular idea of the creativity and artistic endeavour which

Fig. 2.1 American TV imperialism
Alan Wells elaborates how American television imperialism works in Latin America. Latin American television, since its birth, has been dominated by United States finance, companies, technology, programming – and, above all, dominated by New York advertising agencies and practices. There is a very substantial US direct ownership interest in Latin American television stations. 'Worldvision', an ominously titled subsidiary of the US national ABC network, plays a dominant role in Latin America; American advertising agencies not only produce most of the very numerous commercial breaks but also sponsor, shape and determine the whole pattern of programming and importing from the USA. Indeed, 'approximately 80 per cent of the hemisphere's current programs – including *The Flintstones, I Love Lucy, Bonanza* and *Route 66* – were produced in the United States'. This near monopoly of North American television programming within South America distorts entire economies away from 'producerism' and towards 'consumerism'. Madison Avenue picture tube imperialism has triumphed in every Latin American country except Cuba.

J. Tunstall, 1977, discussing A. Wells,
Picture Tube Imperialism, 1972

contribute to the cultural production of films, novels, music, etc. However, if the Marxist view that profitability is the overriding concern of those engaged in cultural production is correct, then the media as industry is an appropriate concept.

1 Film

Cinema as industrial production might be said to characterise Hollywood during the 1930s and 1940s. At the centre was the *studio system*. The major film companies, like MGM, Warner Brothers and United Artists, formed a monopolistic organisation, the Motion Picture Producers and Distributors of America, which effectively prevented any new competition. With strong

Fig. 2.2 **The star system**
Hortense Powdermaker, in her 'anthropological investigation' of *Hollywood, The Dream Factory* (1950), sums this up:

From a business point of view, there are many advantages in the star system. The star has tangible features which can be advertised and marketed – a face, a body, a pair of legs, a voice, a certain kind of personality, real or synthetic – and can be typed as the wicked villain, the honest hero, the fatal siren, the sweet young girl, the neurotic woman. The system provides a formula easy to understand and has made the production of movies seem more like just another business. The use of this formula may serve also to protect executives from talent and having to pay too much attention to such intangibles as the quality of a story or of acting. Here is a standardised product which they can understand, which can be advertised and sold, and which not only they, but also banks and exhibitors, regard as insurance for large profits.

support from the banks, the film companies owned the studios, distribution networks and cinema chains, and thus could ensure their products were always available to the public. Following the control of the American market, they turned to foreign markets, where they quickly gained a dominating position, particularly as they were in a position to offer what was often a technically superior product at a lower price. Even today much of the film making in Europe is dependent upon American finance.

In terms of company assets, the phenomenon of *stars* was a vital aspect of Hollywood film economics. The studios had stars like Bette Davis, Clark Gable and Marilyn Monroe under contract, and thus could be guaranteed so many of their films each year as a form of investment. Stars were especially important for marketing films. They promised audiences a particular and predictable form of pleasure. The history of Hollywood is full of stories of actors and actresses who unsuccessfully tried to break out of the stereotype which their 'star' image represented, the control of the industry to which they belonged being too great (see Fig. 2.2).

The industrial nature of film production could also be seen to shape the structure and content of the end product. The standardised form of storytelling, posing a problem at the beginning and resolving it at the end of the film, was commercially successful, and, as such, opportunity for experimentation or variation was very limited.

Furthermore, films were classified or packaged according to their subject matter, style and conventions, in order to facilitate marketing and promotion to an audience who soon learned what to expect from such film types or genres. These are recognisable to today's audiences, and include musicals, horror films, westerns and gangster films.

2 Television

Hollywood genre films still hold sway over modern audiences, if only through the domestic medium of television. However, television has evolved its own genre within the series format. Such examples include situation comedy, soap opera and current affairs programmes. Series fit very much into the industrial assembly line mode of production as they allow for rationalised planning to produce a uniform end product. Stuart Hood (1980) former controller of BBC television programmes, uses the term 'regular strike' to refer to 'the production rhythm which can be calculated and repeated with ease' (see Reading 1 in Chapter 7).

Profit with commercial television is related to audience size, which means that if a programme is watched by millions of viewers, then the TV companies can sell advertising space at very high prices (see Reading 2).

3 Newspapers

There has been a slow decline in the newspaper industry with the competition between the popular dailies becoming ever more intense. The sex, scandal and sports formula has proved to be the most successful, leading to an increase in uniformity of product. In much the same way that petrol stations attract custom through offering the opportunity to win prizes, so have Britain's popular dailies been involved in attracting readers through offering bingo prizes. (The *Times* current version, Portfolio, merely uses shares instead of ordinary numbers.)

4 Rock music

The music industry is big business, and rock music is marketed in much the same way as other consumer products, even if public taste may not be so stable. 'Brand identity' consists of record companies' artists, who are marketed through advertising, radio airplay, the pop press, etc. Maximising sales is the goal, and this may mean changing the artist's image to appeal to a broader audience, as in the case of Elvis Presley, whose conversion from hillbilly youth rebel to family entertainer in the late 1950s enabled his record company and manager to continue to receive returns on their investment until after his death in 1977 (dying often being a successful way of reviving interest in an artist and reversing declining sales).

Multimarketing

Returning to Murdock and Golding's point concerning the growth of media conglomerates of international scale, then the profitability of the cultural products owned by such companies has been increased through promoting them in more than one form of media outlet. A popular paperback novel may be made into a feature film, on which a television series is based, and the film or TV soundtrack sold as a best selling single or album. It is a case of the music of the TV series of the film of the novel serialised in the magazine . . . Doubtless, readers of this can compile their own list of such multimarketed products (recent examples include representations of ET and Michael Jackson in the form of dolls, teeshirts, gloves, etc.).

The pluralist critique

Writing from the perspective that power in society is not concentrated in the hands of any one group, but is shared by a variety of competing interest groups, the pluralist approach tends to see the media as faithfully reflecting this diversity of interest.

There are several differences of opinion with the Marxist model, notably the following three points:

1 Not all the media organisations are constrained by the profit

motive. The prime example here is *public broadcasting* in Britain and overseas. The BBC is financed by revenue from the public purchase of TV licences, and is thus independent of the need to make a profit and satisfy shareholders. Furthermore, both the BBC and ITV are by law required to broadcast a balance in their output between entertaining, informative and education-al programmes, so preventing a constant diet of soap opera, comedy and sport.

2 *Minority interests are served by the media*, which are often critical of capitalist class interests. This is facilitated both by the structure of broadcasting noted above (and a recent development which might be seen as supportive of the pluralist case is the emergence of Channel 4, committed to giving a voice to groups like ethnic minorities and feminists), and also by the commercial media companies. There are no shortage of publishers, owned by large corporations, who are willing to market the writings of Karl Marx. Much of the rock music in the late 1960s, promoted by the major record companies, exhorted youth to rebel against materialistic values. This leads on to the third point.

3 *Supply meets demand*, i.e. ultimate control rests with the con-sumer; a point often strongly voiced by owners and controllers within media organisations, summed up in the notion that 'we are giving the public what they want'. Any other interpretation would be a case of overestimating the power of the media companies to dictate what their audiences wanted.

The Marxist reply: (2) the influence of profit

Whilst the pluralist critique has shaken the Marxist case in the eyes of many media sociologists, the following points of defence have been made by the Marxists in relation to each of the three main criticisms mentioned above.

1 Public broadcasting cannot stand outside of the economic pressures which affect the commercial TV companies, who need to attract advertisers by winning large audiences. Prior to 1956 the BBC enjoyed a monopoly position in broadcasting and so was not overly concerned with the size of its audience. With the introduction of competition from ITV, the BBC no

longer felt secure about its support from licence fee revenue, which was set by the Government. Stuart Hood (1980) comments that by the late 1950s, the BBC and the Government had unofficially recognised that if the BBC share of the audience fell below 20 per cent, the licence fee would not be justifiable, since when the BBC has fought hard to improve its standings in the ratings from a third to about a half of the audience.

In effect, the BBC is committed to the same goal as ITV, and this is reflected in its scheduling policy and support for popular series, which during the late 1970s succeeded on certain nights of the week in capturing a large majority of the national audience (see Reading 3 for a look at the ratings battle).

2 Some minorities are catered for more than others. The key factor is the wealth of the audience. This point is argued on the basis that the profitability of media products depends on either circulation/sales or advertising revenue. In the case of smaller audiences, if they have above average purchasing power, then advertisers are keen to reach them.

Some influence is particularly evident with the commercial viability of newspapers and magazines. For example, the combined sales of the four British 'quality' (i.e. upmarket) national daily newspapers (*The Times*, the *Telegraph*, the *Guardian* and *The Financial Times*) amounts to about 2¼ million, whilst the top four 'popular' dailies (the *Sun*, the *Mirror*, the *Express* and the *Mail*) together sell 11½ million copies, 400 per cent more than the 'qualities'. Meanwhile, working class papers like the *News Chronicle* and the *Daily Herald*, each with over a million readers, have folded (see Fig. 6.2).

Women's magazines show not only a bias towards the interests of middle class readers, but also women aged 16–34, the age group whose spending power makes them the most attractive to advertisers (see Fig. 6.7).

3 Does the media therefore merely serve a functional purpose of providing the audience with what it demands? Apart from the bias towards more affluent audience groups, the Marxists argue that audience demand cannot be isolated from the influence of supply.

The structure and content of films, TV programmes, newspapers, etc., have tended to stay close to given formulae which are familiar to the audience. Yet often, 'minority' tastes have been discovered to appeal to mass audiences, almost by accident. Snooker and darts are two examples of sports long considered to be of interest to a tiny minority of TV viewers by the programmers. *Monty Python's Flying Circus* began life in a late Sunday night viewing slot usually reserved for arts and religious programmes before its popularity caused a rescheduling to prime viewing time.

Summary of the Marxist case

The Marxist approach emphasises the industrial nature of cultural production with the operation of a 'minimax' policy of taking minimum risk to achieve a maximum audience and hence maximum profit for the large corporate owners, whereas the pluralist approach claims that a much wider range of interests is met by the media than is allowed for in the Marxist model (see Reading 4 for a case study of the rock music industry and pages 60–1 concerning the implications of new technology in broadcasting).

The media as institution

Much of the preceding debate has focused on the economic situation of media production. Little has been said about those studies of the media as institution, i.e. as structured organisations containing professionals with certain types of social relations, practices and values. Are these organisations:

1 well integrated systems within which each member has a clearly defined role contributing to the efficiency of the whole, i.e. the *functionalist* view, or
2 primarily serving the interest of the capitalist class in society, i.e. the *Marxist* view, or
3 comprised of groups and individuals in pursuit of their own goals and interests, often in conflict with those in 'official' authority within and outside media organisations, i.e. the social action view?

This third perspective recognises that the outcome of such conflicts is not predetermined, but is the result of a process of bargaining. Within media institutions there is often a degree of freedom negotiated by media professionals enabling them to engage in cultural production which may be innovatory, or even radical, but at least different from the norm.

Art versus commerce

One of the questions that has hung over cultural production in the press, television, cinemas, etc., in Britain is whether it should be regarded as 'high' culture, i.e. artistic, creative, something of value, or 'low' culture, i.e. vulgar, cheap, disposable. Such aesthetic concerns are relevant here, since those engaged in cultural production often reject the idea that they are merely serving commercial interests and insist that they are in fact creating something of merit.

Such ideals within the media professions may be 'cooled out' by the more cynical senior members but they are still evident in studies of various occupational groups within the media. Within film making there has long been a view held by directors and actors that they are 'creative artists'. Even Hollywood has recognised this side to the film industry, and film critics in the 1960s spent considerable energy in detecting the influence of the 'auteur', or artistic author (i.e. film director), in films which were often dismissed as popular commercial products. A western was now seen as a 'John Ford western', or a thriller became a 'Hitchcock thriller', the personal expression of a 'creative artist'.

British culture has a legacy of upper class elitism and aristocratic paternalism, which has traditionally placed great value on 'art' and 'good taste'. The BBC, to some extent, inherited some of these values in the 1920s. The original Director General, Lord Reith, saw the BBC's responsibility as raising the standards of the audience.

> So the responsibility at the outset conceived, and despite all discouragements pursued, was to carry into the greatest number of homes everything that was best in every department of human knowledge, endeavour and achievement; and to avoid whatever was or might be hurtful. In the earliest years accused of setting out to give the public not what it wanted but what it needed, the answer was that few knew what they wanted, fewer what they needed.
>
> J. Reith, 1949

This elitist view of social responsibility has persisted within the BBC, and acted as a form of resistance to the pressures for a greater proportion of 'popular' commercial output, often resulting in the perpetuation of upper class ideals of taste and achievement. Even within the strict economic constraints of the press, successive owners of *The Times* newspaper have been prepared to withstand its failure to make a profit on the grounds that it has a reputation for 'excellence' and 'tradition', maintaining high journalistic standards.

The elevation of art above commerce has been a means by which those working within the media have managed to achieve a degree of *autonomy*, i.e. self-control and independence from those who own the media but are external to the daily control of media organisations. A second, and closely related, strategy to gain autonomy has been through the idea of professionalism.

Professionalism

Within media occupational groups, professionalism is where the skills and expertise of the occupation are valued as an ideal to which those in the profession should aspire. The particular craft or specialist ability required varies between different media professions, but the importance of such values lies in the way that the claim to professonalism is a means of retaining or negotiating some autonomy within media organisations. In other words, it is a justification for the film director, journalist, actor, etc., resisting 'outside' control, whether from the management, Government or the public, and proceeding according to their own standards.

Within television, **Tom Burns** (1977), on the basis of 300 interviews with BBC staff, found that the *cult of professionalism* was one of the ways that programme makers were able to come to terms with the distance between themselves and the public, whom they are supposed to serve. Another response was to hold to the longstanding Reithian view of 'public service', or simply a 'responsible attitude', whilst a third response was to make limited use of audience ratings as a gauge to their success. Burns found that the three different attitudes were often in conflict, with the newer 'professional' approach tending to undermine the traditional public service attitude by a mixture of referring to fellow professional standards and audience ratings as a way of judging the merit of a programme. Outside pressures, be they political or economic, were considered the problem of management.

Jeremy Tunstall's research (McQuail, 1972) into 207 specialist newsgathering journalists, through observation and unstructured interviews, showed that in contrast to the audience and advertising revenue goals of news organisations newsgathering journalists tended to emphasise a 'non-revenue goal'. Some, like foreign correspondents, were relatively free to produce their stories, whilst others, like crime reporters, were expected to keep in mind the need for maximum readership. Autonomy could be achieved by negotiation, for example, by the need to keep a source confidential as with political correspondents, whose need to protect their close links with politicians can be used to justify the way they present a story.

Other studies of journalists have made the distinction between straight reporters, gathering news through recognised channels, and committed 'investigative' reporters, campaigning on issues or causes (perhaps the most celebrated example being the Watergate journalists, Woodward and Bernstein, on the *Washington Post*, who negotiated the freedom to pursue the exposure of corruption in the White House). On television, institutional space has been given for this style of journalism in programmes like *World in Action*, which are often critical of powerful interest groups.

However, Tunstall noted that the newsgatherers' role was significantly controlled by the news processors, the journalists who edited and presented the stories in the newspapers and magazines. The processors were above all orientated to the audience, i.e. the need for high circulation figures.

The professional and external constraints

There seems to be a good argument to be made for the influence of the autonomous professional working within the media. Yet the example noted above of the pressures of journalists to maximise the audience underlines the point that media organisations can never be seen as isolated from the economic and political structure of society.

1 Regarding news journalists, much has been said of *news values*,

the choice of what is considered 'newsworthy' for readers, such as negativity (bad news is 'good news'), personalities, the unexpected, etc. (see Chapter 3 for further details). These news values can be seen to be ultimately related to what news stories and style of treatment can achieve the biggest audience. Thus we are back to considering profitability and *economic constraints* on the media.

2 Other controls may include *direct intervention by the owners* of the media, as in the case of Rupert Murdoch sacking Harold Evans, the editor of *The Times* for what Evans claimed was basically a conflict over the political policy the newspaper should take.

3 The broadcasting companies, as we have seen, are also subject to commercial pressures, but also *political controls* through the Government's setting of the licence fee for the BBC, and level of taxation of advertising revenue for ITV. Further influence may be exerted by the Government making its criticisms known to the controlling bodies of television, the BBC and IBA governors. In the past the governors of both the BBC and IBA (who are supposedly neutral and independent, but are appointed by the Government, and socially are disproportionally drawn from the upper and middle classes) have banned programmes in response to political requests. Such an example was the (temporary) banning of a BBC documentary *Real Lives* on Northern Ireland in 1985 because it included an interview with a leading IRA member. They have also rejected other requests, defending the TV companies' right to broadcast 'controversial' programmes.

An example of more indirect criticism of TV management can be seen in the following comment made by the Prime Minister in the House of Commons in response to a *Panorama* programme of 1982 deemed less than favourable to the Government's decision to wage war on Argentina over the Falklands:

> I share the deep concern that has been expressed on many sides, particularly about the content of yesterday evening's *Panorama* programme. I know how strongly many people feel that the case for our country is not being put with sufficient vigour on certain – I do not say all – BBC

programmes. The chairman of the BBC has assured us, and has said in vigorous terms, that the BBC is not neutral on this point.

Quoted in R. Harris, 1983

4 Finally; there are *legal restrictions* operating on the media. These range from the laws of libel and obscenity to the Official Secrets Act, which has frequently been invoked to prevent the publication or broadcast of 'leaks' of information from inside Government or discussion of issues sensitive to national security. (For further discussion see Reading 5.)

The question of who controls the media may be seen from a different perspective in the next chapter, when media representations are held up for analysis.

3 Representations

Mirror or distortion?

The *pluralist theory* of power proposes that western industrial societies are essentially democratic. No one group or elite dominates the rest of society, and the balance of power is maintained by the state, the neutral institution of government. Pluralists see the media as being part of that democractic process whereby all points of view and interests are represented within the range of media output. This is seen to spring mainly from the workings of the free market of supply and demand (hence the term *laissez-faire* model) discussed in Chapter 2. For example, the choice of women's magazines reflects the range of women's interests from 'feminine' to feminist.

Much of the public debate surrounding media content has concerned its coverage of political conflict. Even here, the pluralists assert that not only is the whole political spectrum covered, from the *Morning Star* to the *Daily Mail*, but lying somewhere in the middle, in a position of neutrality somewhat similar to that of the state, are the broadcasters, i.e. the BBC and ITV. Their impartiality is based on state regulation, which has created autonomous organisations operating for the *public* interest, the BBC having created this tradition of national responsibility, and later being followed by ITV.

Newspaper journalist claims of letting the facts speak for themselves may well be undermined by public recognition of editorial influence such as the *Sun* proclaiming 'Vote for Maggie' or the *Daily Mirror* 'Vote Labour' on their front pages on election day in June 1983. However, the broadcasting journalist's role is seen as rising above such partisanship to produce balanced and independent coverage. The *professionals* within television and radio largely adhere to this perspective, as can be seen in the following:

The licence requires the BBC to refrain from editorialising;

that is refrain from expressing a point of view of its own on any matter of public controversy or public policy. Careful safeguards have been erected within the BBC to prevent breaches of this rule. For the BBC to take sides in any controversial issue would in any case be contrary to its own long-established policy which, unlike the rule on editorialising has always been self-imposed. The essence of impartiality is balance, and this element, so important to the proper handling of controversial subjects in fact helps the BBC to carry out its obligation to avoid expressions of editorial opinion. Careful attention to balance is one way by which the BBC seeks to ensure that it cannot justly be identified as a supporter of any particular 'line'.

BBC Handbook, 1974

A spell of 25 years in and around BBC News has given me a taste for impartiality and a nose for bias. The capacity to smell out bias was developed as I moved from writing bulletins to editing them. Not that there was much bias to practice on. It did not get a chance to grow, those who rooted it out were its critics inside, not outside, the BBC.

John Crawley, *The Listener*, March 1971

The belief in neutrality and impartiality held by the professionals within broadcasting is also shared by the audience, to judge from the results of research into audience perceptions of news in the media. A typical example is the BBC's Audience Research Report, *News Broadcasting and the Public in 1970*, which noted the following percentages of respondents who considered each of the following to be 'always trustworthy', or 'trustworthy most of the time'.

BBC	86 per cent
ITV	78 per cent
BBC Radio	74 per cent
Newspaper customarily read by respondent	40 per cent
All newspapers	30 per cent

The media thus faithfully reflect the diversity of interest and opinion to be found in society. They are, to use the much quoted metaphors, a 'window on the world' or a 'mirror to reality'.

However, sociologists within the *conflict perspective* do not share this view of the media. In contrast to the pluralist theory of democracy are the theories of a ruling class and elite. Pre-war *mass society* theories suggested that the media was a vital aspect of elite control over the masses, e.g. Nazi propaganda. Eastern European socialist states are often seen as contemporary examples of state control over the population through the media.

Within *Marxism* there has been a similar tradition of the 'conspiracy theory', based on a simple idea that the economic base of society determines the superstructure, i.e. the ruling economic class maintains its position of power through its control of social and political institutions including government and the media. Many of the cruder Marxist accounts of the media have emphasised their 'bias' or *'distortion' of social reality*, suggesting the media's role to be one of a mouthpiece for the ruling class. An often cited example is the stand taken by the BBC during the General Strike of 1926. Lord Reith, the Director General of the BBC, wrote to Baldwin, the Prime Minister, during the strike that, 'Assuming the BBC is for the people, and that the Goverment is for the people, it follows that the BBC must be for the Government in this crisis too.' (Many critics of the media argued that a similar pro-government line was evident in 1984/5 during the miners' strike.) Thus instead of the media reflecting the whole array of social and political interests, as suggested by pluralist accounts, one group, a ruling elite or class, is able to control the media and shape its content in order to protect its interets.

Few media sociologists (including Marxists) today adhere to either of these two approaches. In the 'new' sociology of the media, much work has gone into exposing the myth of the 'window on the world' notion of the media, but the analyses have stopped well short of any simple conspiracy theory. Instead the question has arisen as *how* and *to what extent* does the media serve the interests of the more powerful groups in society?

The manufacture of news

Up to the late 1960s, sociology was dominated by the functionalist perspective, which emphasised consensus as the basis for social order. Regarding the media, it was assumed that it reflected those central values and norms shared by members of society. This assumption was challenged by the *interactionist* perspective, especially those working within the sociology of deviance. The rules of society were not seen as consensual so much as open to interpretation. What was 'normal' to one group, or subculture, may be 'deviant' for another.

Howard Becker (1963) was influential in popularising the *labelling theory* in which he stated: 'Social groups create deviance by making the rules whose infraction constitutes deviance, and by applying those rules to particular persons and labelling them as outsiders.'

This raised the question of which social groups made the rules and how the labelling occurred? Becker failed to develop a general theory of the origins of labelling other than to suggest 'moral entrepreneurs', who tended to be white, male and middle class. However, he did recognise the media's part in the labelling of deviants when examining how the *Reader's Digest* helped to create a social reaction against marijuana smokers following the outlawing of the drug in the USA in 1937.

Following Becker's example, **Stan Cohen** (1972) applied the interactionist perspective to the case of the mods and rockers in the mid 1960s, paying particular attention to the media. Cohen argued that the media were instrumental in labelling youth cultural styles in a stereotyped and negative way, thus creating 'folk devils'. The activities of these folk devils, in this case the conflicts between mods and rockers in British seaside resorts, were then portrayed in such a way as to create a 'moral panic'. Cohen describes this as when 'a condition, episode, person or group of persons emerges to become defined as a threat to societal values and interests'. Examples of moral panics in recent times include soccer hooliganism, student protests and race riots.

The media's role is seen as crucial in structuring public awareness of the issue in terms of the causes, extent and control necessary to contain the 'social problem'. In so doing, they help to *amplify* the problem by creating a social reaction which heightens police activity, court sentencing and public awareness in a vicious escalating circle or *spiral*, which may have little relation to the real situation, i.e. in this case the numbers of mods and rockers involved and the rationale for their behaviour (see Reading 6).

Cohen subsequently co-edited a collection of readings with Jock Young called *The Manufacture of News* (1972), which reinforced the notion that the media was a vital agent in the process of social control. Rather than being a 'mirror on reality', the media helped to *construct* that social reality. The social world could not be assumed to have a fixed, objective reality, but was open to interpretation.

It is therefore logical to ask whose definition of reality is being represented? One approach adopted by the interactionist perspective has been to examine the attitudes and practices of media professionals, particularly those constructing a daily picture of what is happening 'out there': the news journalists.

News values

It is a commonly held misconception that events 'happen', and are then mediated to the public via the printed word and the screen, the mediation being mainly technical, i.e. writing or filming the story. Rarely is newsgathering so simple and direct. A comparison of the front pages of Britain's national newspapers on any day of the week would reveal that journalists *manufacture* news, not in the sense of fabricating it (although some stories may have little basis in reality), but in the sense of making choices about *what* to cover and *how* to cover news. 'News is people. It is people talking and people doing. Committees and Cabinets and courts are people; so are fires, accidents and planning decisions. They are only news because they involve and affect people.' (Harold Evans, *The Practice of Journalism*, Heinemann, London, 1963).

This comment from Harold Evans, former editor of *The Times*, reveals one of the most important news values held by journalists: personalisation, i.e. events are seen as the actions of individuals rather than forces. News values refer to what journalists consider as *newsworthy* (see Reading 7 for a full list of news values and examples from the front pages of two newspapers).

The process of choosing or rejecting stories on the basis of these news values has been referred to as 'gatekeeping', and the journalist most in control of this process is the editor (see Fig. 6.3). Editors fulfil what is essentially a filtering role – selecting or 'opening the gate' for some stories, whilst 'closing the gate' for others, since there is usually an excess of material available to fill limited newspaper or broadcasting space. Therefore, news values may vary according to the editorial policy of a specific newspaper, e.g. the *Sun* may emphasise personalisation and frequency more than *The Times*. Furthermore, technical considerations may also shape news coverage, so that television often includes a story if film is available, or if it is very recent, hence underlining the advantages that it holds over newspapers, who print 'yesterday's' news. Television news editors are especially keen to bring us the news 'as it happens', which means live visual coverage, if possible, or, even more dramatically, a news flash which interrupts the evening's viewing. This helps to strengthen the public idea that 'raw news' is brought direct and unmediated to the audience, an idea which the interactionist perspective has exposed to be mythical. News is the result of a social process guided by the news values held by journalists.

The origins of news values

Journalists do not work in a social vacuum. Whilst it is important to understand how media professionals define the world, it is also necessary to consider the relationship they have with the rest of society. They are not so independent as to be unaffected by certain social and economic forces. *Conflict* sociologists looking at such *structural* influences on the media have distinguished two kinds of such influence.

1 Economic

As outlined in Chapter 2, maximising the audience is a vital goal for most media organisations. A 'good' story is one that is seen as holding the reader's/viewer's attention. Hence the stress on negativity, personalities, drama, at the expense of background detail, complex causes, etc.

Within TV, American companies found that news programmes became more profitable as they tended towards a 'show', using the format of news reading teams, who had individual 'personalities'. British TV news has followed in the same direction with ITV initiating dual news presenters, the BBC having the first female newsreader (Angela Rippon), and newsreaders often being indistinguishable from entertainers.

2 *Cultural*

Events are also more newsworthy if they can be interpreted within a certain framework of values and norms held by journalists, but which are largely derived from outside of media organisations.

> If newsmen did not have available – in however routine a way – such cultural 'maps' of the social world, they could not 'make sense' for their audiences of the unusual, unexpected and unpredicted events which form the basic content of what is 'newsworthy'.
>
> S. Hall, 1978

These cultural 'maps' or assumptions include ideas that society is largely composed of individuals is fundamentally meritocratic, and based on consensus. A functionalist or pluralist perspective would broadly agree with this representation of society, whereas the conflict perspective, especially Marxists, would claim that they are reflecting, if unconsciously, the ideas of those groups who are most powerful in society. Journalists are thus contributing towards the presentation of an *ideological* view of the world.

Ideology

In *The German Ideology* **Marx** wrote that the owners of the means of production, the ruling class, also control the production and distribution of ideas. Thus the ruling economic class is able to rule not by force but through ideas. These ideas function to protect ruling class interests by representing as natural the class relationships of production. For example, under feudalism, a dominant religious idea was that the social order was ordained by God (e.g. the divine right of kings to rule). Under capitalism, ruling class ideology would be found throughout the institutions of family, religion, government, etc., which comprise the 'superstructure' of society. The ideas and social relationships of the 'superstructure' legitimate the economic class relations of production, i.e. the 'base' of society. Thus in politics a belief that government represents the 'national interest' (rather than ruling class interests as Marx believed) is ideological. Ideology then is a way of making sense of the world which produces a *false consciousness* of that world, and so the reality of class domination and exploitation is not recognised. (By using the term 'false consciousness', Marx was intimating that a true or scientific consciousness was possible. Many neo-Marxist writers have argued that all consciousness is to some extent ideological since language can never be neutral.) Therefore, to refer to ideology is to suggest that meanings, beliefs and practices support particular group interests in society, and are not natural or inevitable.

How is ideological domination achieved?

Marx did not make this explicit in his writings and so Marxist writers have had to develop a fuller explanation. This has become essential given that the proletariat have showed less and less evidence of becoming class-conscious and overthrowing capitalism. It is not surprising then that the media should have increasingly come under critical scrutiny by neo-Marxist writers. Some consider it to be the most significant part of the super-structure of advanced capitalist societies. However, the various schools of Marxist thought have been unable to agree on exactly how class domination is achieved through the media. The problem of 'proving' that the media is in fact an instrument of class control has led to debates between Marxists, as well as criticisms by other sociological perspectives, notably pluralism.

Among the main Marxist contributions to the sociology of the media have been the following:

1 The Frankfurt School

They were among the first to suggest that capitalist control of the mass media was the main reason that captalism had survived and flourished in the post-war period. **Herbert Marcuse** (1964) argued that the media helped 'indoctrinate and manipulate, they promote a false consciousness which is immune against its falsehood'. He further claimed that the media deprived art of any critical value by reducing it to mere commerce, e.g. Watney's took the communist slogan 'Red Revolution' and used it in an advertising campaign to promote sales of their 'Red Barrel' beer. Marcuse and others of the Frankfurt School have been criticised for adopting an elitist view of mass (rather than class) society, in which all popular culture is dismissed as 'mass deception', a rather determinist view.

2 Economic determinism

In Chapter 2, we saw how Murdock and Golding (1977) charted the increasing concentration of capitalist ownership of the media. Here the emphasis is very much on the economic base of society determining the media as part of the superstructure. Again, critics have asked does it automatically follow that this produces a particular ideological effect? The owners, with economic, allocative control, are separate from the media professionals, who have day to day operational control, and there is little evidence that the owners directly intervene in such operational control. Therefore, this view has been criticised for being over-determinist.

3 Althusser

The French Marxist, Althusser, used the term 'ideological state apparatus' to refer to the social institutions, including the media, that reproduce ideology in a way that represents capitalism as natural and inevitable. In order to fulfil this function they must be *relatively autonomous* from the direct control of the ruling class, i.e. they must be seen to be independent and self-governing. The fact that TV news is seen as objective and neutral would fit this idea of 'relative autonomy'. Otherwise, the media would not be able to function ideologically, and would be seen as 'biased'. Althusser's work signalled the move away from looking at the economic determinants of the media to concentrate on how the media gives ideological meaning to the world. In particular, Althusser was concerned with how they helped to create an 'imaginery' picture of the real conditions of capitalist production for the subject, i.e. the audience, thus concealing the reality of exploitation. This is achieved by the media offering subjects positions in which they (mis)recognise themselves – as free thinking individuals, members of a democratic society, discriminating consumers, etc.

4 Gramsci

The Italian Marxist, Gramsci's use of the term 'hegemony' has also been influential on Marxist media writers. This refers to the ability of the ruling class to rule by consent, rather than by force, over the working class. This is mainly achieved culturally through education, the media, etc. The media has a central role in producing a 'common sense', which is really a form of ideology. Like Althusser, Gramsci argued for the relative autonomy of the media, and took it further to suggest that the dominant class could never be sure of hegemonic order, but rather it had to be struggled for against opposition, especially when capitalism passed through one of its periodic crises (e.g. an economic depression).

Both Althusser and Gramsci have been influential in directing attention toward the ideological role of the media, but mainly at a theoretical level. To understand better its working in practice within the media, we will consider the work of two sociological research centres in Britain.

Centre for Contemporary Cultural Studies (CCCS)

The CCCS in Birmingham University, formerly headed by Stuart Hall, has produced a wealth of material on the media since the early 1970s. The main thesis has concerned the *ideological effect* of the media, which is to shape and organise consensus in what is essentially a class divided society. The media's (especially TV's) perceived status as neutral, impartial and balanced actually works to create this effect, since it serves to endorse the political system as it stands, i.e. a two party parliamentary system. Within news and current affairs, balance ensures that there is always a two-sided dialogue, and, by inference, that the truth lies somewhere in between. This also means that issues are debated within certain boundaries (BBC's *Question Time* might be considered typical of how the debate is framed within the selection of the invited guests who make up the panel). Groups falling outside the parliamentary system are labelled illegitimate, extremist, undemocratic, etc., e.g. the IRA or Greenham women peace protestors. The media's role then is to help *set the agenda* to decide which issues will be examined within what is taken to be a framework of consensus, i.e. the 'national interest'.

In their work, *Policing the Crisis* (1978), Hall and his colleagues apply Gramsci's concept of hegemony to post–war Britain. They argue that following the period of stability and affluence of the 1950s and early 1960s Britain entered a period of economic and social crisis when public consent seemed to be weakening (especially in industrial relations), thus threatening ruling class hegemony. In order to win support for stronger powers to control this crisis, it was represented as a crisis of law and order. Hall contends that various separate social issues were transformed into 'moral panics' (e.g. student protests, picketing, mugging) and interconnected so as to appear to be one common problem, the breakdown of law and order, paving the way for changes leading to stronger state control. The media's contribution to this sequence is the access it provides for the *primary definers* of the crisis, those considered legitimate spokespeople, i.e. the government and agencies of social control, the police, courts, etc. These are the people with power, and to whom the media naturally turn to make sense of the world, given their own commitment to remain detached and impartial (see Reading 8 on mugging and the media).

The Glasgow Media Group (GMG)

In their first two publications, *Bad News* (1976) and *More Bad News* (1980), the group reported the results of their systematic analysis of six months of TV news programmes from January to June 1975. *Bad News* is concerned with industrial relations coverage, and the group found that certain workers received disproportionate attention. A half of all industrial stories in the bulletins concerned just three industries – vehicle building, transport and communication and public administration – yet several major disputes in the engineering and shipbuilding industries went virtually unreported. What was more remarkable was that in terms of the stories covered there was great similarity between the BBC and ITN. This suggests that they hold common assumptions about the coverage of industrial disputes.

Why were those industries selected for prominent coverage? The authors suggest that the car industry typified a dominant view about strike-prone workers, who, despite high wages, are not content, and also the problem of economic survival for an industry subject to international competition. The emphasis on transport and communication and public administration was thought to reveal a concern for the inconvenienced consumer of goods and services. This was largely confirmed by a case study of a thirteen week dustmen's strike in Glasgow, which from the outset was treated primarily as a health hazard story (yet it was not until after seven weeks of the dispute that Glasgow Corporation announced a health hazard existed), thus ignoring the real strike cause, that of pay.

In this way, the media is seen as structuring industrial relations stories to fit a dominant consensual view that uninterrupted production is a 'good thing' and that strikes are disruptive and harmful. In *More Bad News* this conclusion is reinforced in the analysis of the language that TV uses to represent industrial disputes (see Fig. 6.4). The language is skewed toward management, who exercise control as of right, whereas the workers' action is often made to seem lacking in motive, and so appears as irrational or simply militant. The main theme of this book is how the problem of inflation (which was quite high in 1975) was perceived by TV news. The main government interpretation, that it was due to excessive wage claims, was also the main explanation offered by TV. Statements which contradicted this view were more likely to be challenged by reporters (see Reading 9 for a summary of their findings).

THE CCCS AND GMG RESEARCH: A SUMMARY

1 Both the CCCS and GMG have concentrated on the way in which media representations are *ideological*, they tend toward producing a view of the world which helps to disguise the nature of class-based inequality in society. Being mainly *Marxist* in their approach, it is not surprising that they regard this ideology as serving to maintain the interests of those with economic power, in perpetuating a capitalist economic system (hence the GMG's focus on industrial conflict and the media).

2 In following the tradition of neo-Marxists like Gramsci and Althusser, they have recognised the *relative autonomy* of the media, i.e. they do not act as propaganda agents or mouthpieces for the capitalist class, but media professionals have some freedom in which to produce newspapers, TV programmes, etc. In this way, it cannot be assumed that the media will automatically defend such class interests. A careful analysis of content is necessary in search of its ideological meaning.

Therefore, it may be possible for messages opposed to ruling class interests to be produced. Periodically the BBC and ITV are attacked by those in power for allowing 'illegitimate', and possibly subversive, views to be presented, e.g. TV programmes in which the IRA have been allowed to present their case (see the pluralist argument in Chapter 2).

3 This leads on to the popular Marxist concept of *dominant ideology*. Other ways of interpreting the world may get expressed, but these are given far less prominence, or are presented less coherently, due to a lack of power in society.

In recent years, a strong case has been made for there being forms of structured inequality between groups other than social classes. These include *gender*, *race* and *age*.

Patriarchal ideology

Feminism has made a large impact on sociology in the last decade. Although, as with Marxism, there are differences within feminist theory, feminists share a view that societies are characterised by male domination (patriarchy) over women. This domination enables men to gain at women's expense, particularly in the home, where women are tied to a domestic role which exploits them (e.g. housework as a duty), and restricts their opportunities to succeed in the world of paid work.

The question that feminists have tried to answer is why women do not rebel against this oppression. Like Marxists trying to explain the failure of the working class to rebel, they have turned to the concept of ideology. Patriarchal ideology works to represent gender roles, with the division between man as economic provider and woman as emotional provider in the home, as 'natural' and inevitable, rather than a product of male power.

Various studies have identified a patriarchal ideology running through the media, whether in children's comics, adverts or the cinema. Angela McRobbie's account of the ideology of *Jackie*, the teenage girl's weekly, is a good example (see Fig. 3.1).

Women's and girls' magazines are seen as crucial in defining a 'woman's world'. They exist for every stage of growth, from child to adolescent to young single adult to married woman in a way that isn't parallelled by men's magazines. These exist solely

Fig. 3.1 **The ideology of *Jackie***
What, then, are the central features of *Jackie* in is so far as it presents its readers with an ideology of adolescent femininity? First it sets up, defines and focuses exclusively on 'the personal', locating it as the sphere of *prime* importance to the teenage girl. It presents this as a totality – and by implication all else is of secondary interest to the 'modern girl'. Romance problems, fashion, beauty and pop mark out the limits of the girl's concern – other possibilities are ignored or dismissed.

Second, *Jackie* presents 'romantic individualism' as the ethos, *par excellence*, for the teenage girl. The *Jackie* girl is alone in her quest for love; she refers back to her female peers for advice, comfort and reassurance *only* when she has problems in fulfilling this aim. Female solidarity, or more simply the idea of girls together – in *Jackie* terms – is an unambiguous sign of failure. to achieve self-respect, the girl has to escape the 'bitchy', 'catty', atmosphere of female company and find a boyfriend as fast as possible. But in doing this she has not only to be individualistic in outlook – she has to be prepared to fight ruthlessly – by plotting, intrigue and cunning, to 'trap her man'. Not surprisingly, this independent-mindedness is short-lived. As soon as she finds a 'steady', she must renounce it altogether and capitulate to *his* demands, acknowledging his domination and resigning herself to her own subordination.
A. McRobbie, '*Jackie*, an ideology of adolescent feminity',
in B. Waites *et al.*, 1982

for leisure interests of all age male groups, an indicator of the difference (and greater freedom) of their role. *Jackie*, as a teen magazine, is especially important in being the most popular girls' weekly at an age when potentially they have the least restrictions on their leisure. In common with other popular women's magazines, the emphasis is on the female as someone who is looked at rather than who does things, and romance as being the meaning of life. The main conventions of *Jackie* stories all revolve around romantic themes, whether it is in history – a Roman falling for a slave girl, or a more modern fantasy of

> **Fig. 3.2 Blacks as traditionally represented by Hollywood**
> Boskin quotes a description of the Sambo characteristics provided by Robert Penn Warren.
> He was the supine, grateful, humble, irresponsible, unmanly, banjo-picking, servile, grinning, slack-jawed, docile, dependent, slow-witted, humorous, child-loving, child-like, water-melon-stealing, spiritual-singing, blamelessly fornicating, happy-go-lucky, hedonistic, faithful black servitor who sometimes might step out of character long enough to utter folk wisdom or bury the family silver to save it from the Yankees.
>
> Hartmann and Husband, 1974

meeting the boy of your dreams. In fact, dreaming is part of the message – that it is normal and 'feminine' to be passive.

Racist ideology

Inequalities between racial groups, i.e. white supremacy, have been well documented in official statistics and various social surveys. Racial discrimination has been proven to be a major causal factor, and this has been closely linked to *racism*, an ideology of white racial superiority over blacks. Having its roots in the colonial past of Western Europe, this ideology explains white rule in Africa and Asia in terms of white culture as 'civilised' or 'developed' and black culture as 'primitive' or at worst 'savage'. Whilst these images may seem dated, they can still be found in films made during the era of the British Empire, or in the USA during the period of racial segregation in the deep south (see Fig. 3.2 for an example of the cruder stereotypes).

The *Black and White Minstrel Show* was still reinforcing this image on the BBC in the 1960s. Within contemporary TV, these images have been recycled, notably in situation comedy series like *It ain't half hot, Mum*, *Love thy Neighbour* or *Till Death us do Part*. It is debatable whether the white racist sentiments held by Alf Garnett work as a parody or reinforce traditional myths.

Hartmann and Husband's (1974) analysis of the press coverage of race in Britain further underlines the dominance of negative ideas about blacks and ethnic groups. The reportage was in terms of blacks as a threat or a problem within the context of racial conflict, immigration, inner city decay, unemployment and crime. As with the GMG and CCCS (who themselves pointed out that mugging was labelled as a crime typical of black youths), the authors refer to the ability of those in power to define the terms of the debate, to set the agenda.

The above examples by no means exhaust the ways in which recent researchers have identified the ideological meaning of media representations. For example, TV popular entertainment, like situation comedy or soap opera, has been questioned for its uncritical affirmation of the middle class nuclear family as the centre of social normality.

Ruling class ideology?

It is clear that once it is acknowledged that the media has a degree of *relative autonomy* from ruling class interest, then there can be no certainty that it will simply reflect a ruling class ideology. Instead, many conflict sociologists have tended to prefer the term *dominant ideology* allowing for the possibility of:

1 alternative ideologies, like patriarchy, and even
2 content which is *opposed* to the dominant ideology.

A good example here might be *rock music*. The reistance of youth to adult authority has been channelled through the music and style of various youth subcultures for the last thirty years. Perhaps the most explicit expression of this was the youth counter culture of the late 1960s, when much of the music was either protesting against war ('All you need is love'), or encouraging drug consumption. More recent examples might include the cynicism and nihilism of punk rock, and the black consciousness of reggae music.

Methodology – how is ideology discovered?

How exactly can the sociologist analyse the meaning of media representations? Studies mentioned above have used a range of methods, but fall roughly into two main approaches:

1 Content analysis

This involves a systematic counting and description of a large area of media content. The researcher identifies a set of categories, and then sets out to record the frequency with which each category occurs within a given area of the media. As such, it claims to be objective, being based on hard empirical data which can be checked.

The GMG made much use of content analysis, for example, in counting the amount of coverage given to particular strikes which occurred within the same period in order to show a misrepresentation of reality. Other researchers have counted the frequency with which blacks and women are represented in different occupations compared to whites and men (see Fig. 6.5). The results often confirm negative cultural stereotyping of groups like women, ethnic minorities and the elderly, or show how the media give a distorted view of reality, for example, in over-representing the amount of violence that exists in society. In this way, content analysis can be a valuable corrective to the individual's selective consumption of TV programmes or magazines.

CRITICISMS OF CONTENT ANALYSIS
1 There is a danger that the events will simply confirm a hypothesis because of the way the categories have been chosen, in the same way that a questionnaire often determines the answers due to the way the questions are worded. Martin Harrison's (1985) re-examination of the TV broadcasts analysed by the GMG suggests they may be guilty of selective use of the evidence to support their own (Marxist) critical theory of television news.
2 In monitoring the media for certain categories of representation, say violence, then the meaning of that representation may be misunderstood, because it is taken out of context. It may well be that in, for example, *Minder* or *The Avengers* (for older readers), each episode contains a certain quota of violence, but taken within the structure of the programme it is essentially ritualistic and humorous rather than 'real' violence.

This suggests the need for an approach which is more sensitive to the particular ways in which the media communicates messages. This approach is semiology.

2 Semiology

This refers to the study of the meaning of signs. It derives from linguistics, and attempts to understand how language, as a system of signs or code, communicates meaning. Language and other forms of communication are structured according to certain rules which are understood culturally (hence being literate means understanding those rules). What interests semiologists, and indeed sociologists, is the way that signs (like words or images) help us to make sense of the world, how they *signify* reality.

Roland Barthes, a French semiologist, distinguished between the way signs denote and connote meaning. *Denotation* refers to the simple and obvious meaning of a sign, e.g. a photograph of a street denotes that street. However, photographs are not simply a mechanical reproducton of reality. There is a process of human intervention in selecting how to photograph a street. This includes whether to use black and white or colour film, focus sharply or softly, etc. Black and white film, for example, may give the impression that it is an old photograph, or may make the street seem bleak. Barthes calls this *connotation*, the cultural meaning inferred in the sign. It is not fixed, but is open to interpretation. A red flag could connote danger or communism. Through convention and use it has become *symbolic* of these ideas. *Myth* is the term Barthes uses to refer to a chain of ideas associated with a sign. By myth he doesn't mean they are false, but that they represent cultural ways of making sense of the world. A picture of a white man wearing a white coat and standing next to a statistical diagram symbolises science – objective, factual (and white/masculine) knowledge, whereas a picture of a black man in exotic garments standing next to a large pot of boiling water over a fire symbolises primitiveness or even sorcery and witchcraft. These are cultural codes which we use to give meaning to the world, and which can be seen as ideological, the above being examples of both racist and sexist ideology.

In a novel, words (signs) are organised and structured to

signify meaning within the text. Similarly, media 'texts' contain sign systems or audio-visual codes which can be sociologically *decoded* to reveal the underlying ideology. (For a semiological interpretation of the news see Reading 10.) When certain codes become popularly recognised they are referred to as *genres*. These include such cinematic forms as the 'musical', the 'gangster', and the 'western'. We recognise the western by certain visual signs like the cowboy clothes, the landscape, etc., and by narrative themes of the hunt for the outlaw, civilising the west, etc. The western's ideological messages concern American history – the Indian as savage and aggressive, the triumph of law and order, etc. Genres then may carry certain meanings which limit how a given text can be interpreted. We may find it difficult to make sense of a dramatic political speech in the context of a situation comedy other than as a send-up of politics. (For a semiological analysis of advertising, which uses quite complex codes, see Reading 11.)

It is not correct to see semiology as necessarily an alternative to content analysis. The two approaches may be, and have been, used together (the GMG attempted some limited decoding of TV signs). It is a matter of emphasis – analysing the categorising of *overt* or *manifest* meaning of the content, or analysing the *covert* or *latent* meaning of the form and structure of the content.

CRITICISMS OF SEMIOLOGY (AS IDEOLOGY)

1 Semiology is not a systematic or comprehensive method, and as such is open to the accusation of being unrepresentative (or unreliable) in its results. It is possible that deviant cases containing radical or subversive meaning may be overlooked.

2 The meaning of the text, which is revealed by semiological/ sociological decoding, cannot be assumed to be the same meaning decoded by the audience. Will they obtain the same interpretation of a TV programme? (see the next chapter on the audience). Furthermore, the fact that cultural codes are constantly changing points to a struggle or *negotiation* over their meaning. Blacks in America in the 1960s sought to transform the meaning of the word 'black' from something threatening and negative to something powerful and positive – 'black is beautiful'.

4 Audience

The relationship between the media and its audience has been debated throughout this century. In following this debate historically, it is possible to see how sociology's approach to the media has passed through different stages. To simplify matters these can be divided into three periods: from 1900 until the Second World War; from the war until the early 1960s; and the last twenty years. Politicians, advertisers, trade unionists, minority groups, etc., have all had their say, but outside of sociology it has perhaps been psychology which has had most influence on the academic debate.

The media as 'hypodermic needle'

In the period between 1900 and the 1930s, there developed a widespread belief that the media had tremendous power in society. It was felt that society had changed from one in which social relationships were personal, intimate and communal (characterised by Ferdinand Tönnies as *gemeinschaft* society) to one in which relationships were impersonal, anonymous and isolated (*gesellschaft*). This change was thought to be caused by the twin processes of industrialisation and urbanisation. The new large scale and densely populated cities were part of a growing *mass society*. In rather pessimistic tones, individuals were now seen as part of a rootless mass, no longer belonging to a close-knit social community. The newly emergent mass media, starting with newspapers and then cinema and radio, was seen as an all-powerful means of communicating with this mass of isolated individuals.

The audience was very much viewed as being acted upon by the media in a one-way process. This 'hypodermic' or (as referred to in the USA) 'magic bullet' effect was thought to be uniform and direct. Psychologically, it reflects a *behaviourist* view of learning. Media messages act as strong stimuli on the individual's emotions and sentiments, causing them to respond in a determined way, i.e. creating changes in thought and action.

These views were not based on any social scientific evidence, but on widespread speculation about the media's role in certain social changes of the time. Government propaganda in the First World War, followed by Soviet and fascist propaganda in the 1920s and 1930s, reinforced the belief that political elites could manipulate masses through the media. Their experience of fascist rule in Nazi Germany contributed to the Frankfurt School's critical approach toward what they saw as a mass popular culture which caused a loss of individual freedom or creative thinking, and instead created 'false needs' (consumerism). The mass media, as part of the 'culture industry', was particularly held as responsible.

Similar conclusions, albeit from a very different academic standpoint, were reached by literary critics in England. In an influential text, *Mass Civilization and Minority Culture* (1930), F. R. Leavis argued that popular culture was vulgarly commercial, pandering to the lowest common tastes. The dominance of market forces (i.e. the profit motive) in culture meant that standards had fallen, and civilisation was under threat. Leavis and his followers thought that an appreciation of English literature would be the only means of preserving high cultural standards. There followed a tradition of English teaching in schools which at best was, and still is, suspicious of popular media products like paperback best selling novels, or TV entertainment.

This elitist view of the masses, but especially the working class, as being susceptible to the power of the media still persists today. The pre-war period saw the first of many *moral panics* concerning the media's harmful influence on those viewed as most likely to be corrupted: young people. The cinema was an early target, criticised by moralists like Leavis, who thought it represented the worst in popular entertainment, involving 'surrender under conditions of hypnotic receptivity to the cheapest emotional appeals' (quoted in Pearson, 1983). Apart from the fears of becoming 'Americanised', i.e. concerned with material pleasures, vulgarity, etc., Hollywood films were accused of leading young people toward criminal behaviour through 'copycat' imitation of the villains portrayed on the screen. Since then, there have been similar claims made about children's comics, radio and TV detective thrillers, and, most recently, 'video nasties'. Many even attributed the urban riots in Britain's cities during the summer of 1981 to teenagers copying what they had seen on TV news.

Criticisms

1 Underlying all the accounts of harmful media effects is an assumption that there was once a 'golden age' when such influences did not exist, and when all was social harmony and integration. Yet, as Geoffrey Pearson points out, many of these sorts of claims were made as far back as the eighteenth century with respect to public fairs and other 'debased' amusements. Such romantic nostalgia is mythmaking, and allows the media to be blamed for 'modern' social problems.

2 From a strictly empirical point of view, no concrete research was undertaken before the 1930s to discover whether the media did cause any such effects. Mass society theorists were simply speculating about the media's influence in society.

3 As will be seen, subsequent research has shown the 'hypodermic' or 'magic bullet' theory to be far too deterministic – it assumes that the audience passively absorbs media messages, which is a very simplistic view of learning, and ignores the social context of the audience in consuming the media.

Effects research: psychology

During the 1920s, psychology and sociology began to adopt scientific techniques of research to the study of human thinking and behaviour, e.g. the measurement of attitudes. At the same time, public concern over the possible harmful effects of the media was mounting. It seemed logical then that the social sciences should try and measure these effects. The Payne studies, published in 1932, were just such an attempt. These evaluated the effects of cinema on audiences and the results seemed to confirm some of the critics' worst fears – films stimulated children to commit acts of delinquency and crime, changed attitudes, disturbed sleep, etc. Soon after, there was a research report detailing how badly frightened and disturbed many people had been following just one radio programme in the USA, the *War of the Worlds*, which was presented in the form of a news bulletin claiming America had been invaded by Martians.

Since the war, there have been further surveys which have claimed to find a direct connection between exposure to media content and changes in attitude and behaviour. These have mainly involved psychologists, who have used the *laboratory method* of investigation in attempting to obtain scientific results. The experimental group is subjected to some specific content, usually violent or sexual, whereas a control group is shown something neutral, and the groups' responses are compared (e.g. observing their social behaviour afterwards). A typical recent example would be the work of **Eysenck and Nias** (1978), who claim that TV violence directly causes violence among juveniles. Quite often the findings of these reports have led to censorship. For example, in the 1930s, partly as a result of the Payne studies, the film studios introduced a production code which, among other things, ruled that a crime must not be presented attractively and that 'the sanctity of marriage and the home shall be upheld'. In the 1950s it was children's comics that came under scrutiny, and most recently the moral panic over 'video nasties' led to the passing of restrictive legislation.

Criticisms

1 With the laboratory method, the question arises as to whether subjects may respond in a way which is designed to please the experimenter.

2 The content of media representation is not easy to categorise, so that violence, for example, may vary from *Tom and Jerry*, to news reports of violence on the picket lines, to TV crime series like *The A Team* and *Kojak*. The meaning of the content is to some degree determined by the context of the form in which it appears.

3 The subjects are removed from their social context, and are assessed as atomised individuals. However, their consumption of the media, and engagement in activities like violence, usually takes place within a social environment, which varies considerably from group to group. (For a further discussion, see Reading 12).

Effects research: sociology (1940s–60s)

Whilst some of the earlier reports like the Payne studies noted the need to take into account the social context which went with watching the cinema, reading comics, etc., it was not until the publication of *The People's Choice* in 1948 that a major shift in assessing the media's effects began. The authors, **Lazarsfeld**, **Berelson and Gaudet**, were trying to discover what influence the media had on voting behaviour in American elections. They used a panel sample, whereby subjects were interviewed regularly over a six month period leading up to the election, so that the effects of the media during the campaign could be measured. The most significant finding was that more than half of the voters had already selected their candidate before the interviewing began. Their predisposition to vote a particular way was then reinforced through a tendency to buy only those newspapers or listen to those radio programmes which supported their views, a process of *selective exposure*. Very few were open to conversion, and those that were undecided did not show much interest in the campaign. It was also discovered that personal discussion was of much greater importance in determining political views. 'Opinion leaders' were singled out as being especially influential. These were trusted people, who were actively interested in politics, and who did much to interpret media information for their immediate social group, a process the authors referred to as a *two step flow*.

The 'hypodermic' model of communication had been replaced by one that emphasised the audience as:

1 already having well-formed attitudes
2 consciously selecting and interpreting messages (what psychologists call cognition)
3 belonging to social groups rather than being isolated individuals.

⧎The overall conclusions seemed to be that the media's 'effect' on the audience was one of reinforcement rather than change. ⧉ (For a summary of political effects research see Reading 13.) Instead of seeing the media as an all-powerful force working on the audience, the emerging view was that the media only had limited effects, since the audience was active not passive.

Criticisms

The main objection to the above conclusions (particularly from the *conflict* perspective) concerns the belief that media effects can be measured within a short period of time, e.g. an election campaign, and through an examination of specific programme 'messages', e.g. current affairs political coverage. This ignores the longer term 'effect' of the whole range of ideological content (covered in Chapter 3), which is to be found within a variety of forms of media production like TV soap opera or situation comedy. These may have a significant part to play in shaping the political consciousness of the audience.

Most sociologists, however, are agreed that the effects re-search was of value in pointing to the active role of the audience in selecting from, and using, the media in order to fulfil certain needs.

Uses and gratifications

There is now quite a long history of studies detailing the appeals of media consumption for the audience. **Blumler and Katz's** research, *The Uses of Mass Communication* (1974) is typical of the uses and gratifications approach. They attempted to discover the goals of TV viewing from the viewers themselves. During unstructured group discussions they listed the main motives for viewing as suggested by respondents, then compiled a list of the most frequently mentioned statements, and submitted this to a cross section of TV viewers to discover the main uses and gratifications categories.

The needs which TV most satisfied were found to be:

1 *diversion* – forms of escape or emotional release from everyday pressures
2 *personal relationships* – companionship for lonely people, or a source of conversation
3 *personal identity* – being able to compare one's life with the programme content, exploring personal problems and rein-forcing personally held values
4 *surveillance* – source of information about the world.

(See Fig. 6.6 for a uses and gratifications analysis of TV quiz shows.)

In taking audience goals and orientation as the starting point for research, uses and gratifications can be placed within the *interpretive* perspective. No assumption is made about how media content affects the audience, nor is this attempted. Indeed, the strategy is not far removed from market research undertaken by media organisations seeking to discover their audience, and where needs are not being met. As such, it also fits into a *pluralist* view of the media – supply meets demand, the consumer selects the desired product from the media supermarket shelf. It is clear that many TV programmes, newspapers, magazines, etc., appeal to distinct social groups (see Fig. 6.7 for a profile of women's magazine readers).

Criticisms

By suggesting that individuals have certain 'needs', the theory comes very close to a kind of 'psychological functionalism', i.e. the media exists to meet those universal needs. However, critics have posed the following related questions:

1 Are not those 'needs' to some extent determined by learning to enjoy or make use of what is available, i.e. a choice ultimately made not by the audience but by media producers? Supply shapes demand.

2 Can it be taken for granted that the audience is aware of the pleasures inherent in media representations? Psychologists influenced by the work of Freud have suggested that media images and symbols may appeal to an individual's *unconscious desires* which have been repressed since childhood. This particularly applies to sexuality in the various forms in which it is expressed in films, magazines, etc.

3 Are these uses and gratifications individual needs or social/subcultural group needs? If the latter, then it becomes much more problematic as to how different social groups may r use of the same content.

Despite these doubts, most sociologists now re' that the audience may use and make sense c' tions in ways that cannot be assumed by content or its source.

The 'new' view of the audience

By the late 1960s, media sociologists were working with very different ideas about the audience. They had more modest expectations regarding the discovery of any 'effects'; the audience was now seen as active not passive; and the long term effects of ideological content were being appraised.

Furthermore, *social structural changes* were having their impact on sociological media analysis:

> it can be argued that the basic reason behind the shift in the argument about the effects from a powerful to a limited to a more powerful mode is that the social world was being transformed over this period . . . Powerful effects of communication were sensed in the thirties because the Depression and the political current surrounding the war had created a fertile seed for the production of certain kinds of effects. Similarly, the normalcy of the fifties and sixties led to a limited effects model. In the late sixties a period of war, political discord and inflation combined to expose the social structure in fundamental ways and to make it permeable by the media of communication.

> J. Carey quoted in McQuail, 1983

It has been argued that such social change has contributed to a combination of more *audience dependency* on the media for information, and an attempt by those with power to use the media as a means of social control and influence. Television, in particular, has seemed to become more significant as a source of knowledge given the way social institutions like government, education and religion have tried to gain access to the airwaves. Sociologists like **Jay Blumler** have pointed to the increasing prominence of TV as a medium of political communication. He has argued that this has helped to 'activate' the audience politically by providing far more political information than they have ever received before. What is more, given TV's more 'balanced' political coverage than newspapers', it has reduced the viewers' opportunity to be exposed only to those political views already held, (like a conservative supporter may be doing in buying the *Daily Express*). The overall effect, Blumler thinks, has been to make viewers more politically sceptical, and thus added to the growing unpredictability of voters at election time.

Another writer who thinks that TV has become more important as a source of information on social reality is George Gerbner. In a kind of 'mass society mark 2 model', he proposes that the audience has become increasingly isolated, and reliant on TV for information about the outside world. As such, TV has a *cultivation effect*, i.e. shaping beliefs and consciousness of social reality. By using content analysis, Gerbner has shown how TV 'distorts' reality, especially in portraying the world as a violent place. He has followed this up with an audience survey in which he has shown that 'heavy' viewers (who watch an above average amount of TV) are much more likely to overestimate the real amount of violence in society (i.e. as revealed in official statistics) – an effect he calls the 'cultivation differential'.

Gerbner's work has been questioned on the following grounds:

1 What is the precise definition of a heavy or light viewer?
2 Do heavy viewers already tend to have a more distorted view of reality regardless of their TV viewing?
3 What about the effects of social background, subculture, etc.?

A study which partly confirms the view that the media does help to form people's views, but also tries to allow for personal experience of social reality is Hartmann and Husband's *Racism and the Mass Media* (1974). In this they tried to weigh up the relative importance of the media as opposed to personal situation in determining attitudes towards race in Britain (for a summary of their findings see Reading 14).

The Centre for Contemporary Cultural Studies (CCCS) has also considered the question of how audiences make sense of, or *decode*, media output within their various social contexts. Borrowing from semiology, **Stuart Hall** has suggested that media forms (or texts) are encoded ideologically with a *preferred meaning* to be understood by the audience, but that there is a degree of freedom for various audience decodings or interpretations of the text content (the signs). These decodings may be related to specific social situations. For example, in the working class, they might range from complete acceptance of the dominant ideology contained in a TV programme to a rejection, or oppositional decoding, of the programme. The acceptance might be found within affluent, privatised working class areas, whereas the oppositional reading might come from the more traditional 'proletarian' working class areas, especially among committed trade unionists.

To test this idea, **David Morley**, in *The 'Nationwide' Audience* (1980), interviewed various social groups about their responses to *Nationwide*, the BBC's weekday current affairs magazine of the 1970s. Groups tending towards a dominant reading (i.e. those seen by Morley as closest to *Nationwide*'s own values) included bank managers and apprentices, whilst those rejecting *Nationwide* and producing an oppositional reading included black further education students and shop stewards. In between (having a 'negotiated' reading) were teacher training and university students, and trade union officials. By interviewing groups of viewers, Morley did not fall into the trap of seeing the TV audience as composed of isolated individuals. Nevertheless, there is a problem that group interviews tend towards a common view which suppresses individual variations. The main question mark against the CCCS encoding/decoding model concerns who decides what is the dominant or preferred reading of a media text – the sociologist or the audience? Morley categorises the answers according to *his* understanding of *Nationwide*, from a mainly Marxist perspective. The question persists as to how far the media constructs social reality for the audience?

5 Social policy

The key issue concerning media policy has always been one of control. How much control should be exercised over the media, and by whom? Given that the media has such a vital role to play in the flow of information in society, it might be expected that there would be clearly defined regulations governing its operation. However, in Britain this is not the case.

Policy traditions

Partly because the media has developed during different historical periods, e.g. newspapers in the nineteenth century, radio and cinema in the 1920s and television since the war, there has never been a coherent central policy which embraces all the media at once. Each has established its own separate policy tradition. The press, for example, has a long history of being defended from outside interference on the grounds of protecting 'the freedom of the press', whereas broadcasting from the start was subject to state control. Rarely has there been any attempt to view the different media as interrelated. **Jeremy Tunstall** (1983) estimates that there are some thirty public bodies involved in setting and carrying out media policy ranging across many government departments like the Home Office, Treasury, Foreign Office and Department of Education and Science. In effect, Tunstall says the nearest thing to a media minister is the Prime Minister, the only person who is able to coordinate all these departments. (This is in contrast to many other Western European countries who bring all media under a single government department of communications or culture.)

Despite the diversity of policy approaches towards different media there are some common features. Tunstall argues that the overriding principle has been one of minimum legislation and voluntarism. For example, media 'policing' organisations like the Press Council or the Broadcasting Complaints Commission, have very limited powers. These are usually restricted to instructing newspapers or the BBC or ITV to publicise any complaints made which are thought to be legitimate (in the case of the press these can be ignored). This non-involved attitude is also reflected in the appointments to the Royal Commissions and committees established by parliament to investigate the role of the media. The members are usually a mixture of 'distinguished' amateurs drawn from academia, business and public life, and they tend to produce reports characterised by a mixture of conservatism, compromise and references to abstract ideals like freedom and democracy (see Fig. 5.1).

This underlines the other main principle of media policy, that of consensus – the avoidance of any visible political interference in the daily running of the media, and protection of its independence to pursue its goal of meeting the needs of the audience. This particularly applies to *broadcasting*, whose *public service* role has been enshrined in the terms of the charters under which the BBC and IBA operate.

Consequences

The lack of any clear centrally directed policy has meant that government initiated change has been very slow. Policy making cycles since the war have averaged twelve years, moving from an enquiry phase in which vague recommendations are made by a committee or commission, to a political phase in which a few watered-down proposals emerge, to an operational phase during which the real meaning of the policy is decided at institutional level. Thus, for example, Channel 4 was first discussed in the Annan Committee of 1974–7, and they ended up advocating an open broadcasting authority. The basis for this authority was so inadequately conceived that eventually it was awarded to ITV, and the actual shape and policy of Channel 4 was only just becoming clear in 1985.

The weaknesses of media policy have meant that key decisions have been left to both the owners and professional controllers of the media (the question of which has greater power is discussed in Chapter 2). The unchecked growth of media conglomerates is one consequence. Despite the existence of a monopolies commission designed to prevent excessive market domination by a few large companies, mergers and takeovers have continued at a

Fig. 5.1 **The issue of media freedom**
Some of the most elementary principles – such as freedom – are not defined and some of the simplest available policy devices, such as taxation, are not co-ordinated. Discussions of media 'freedom' implicitly make quite different assumptions about quite similar situations. In films 'freedom' is seen as a problem for one individual, the director, against largely commercial forces. In the press the focus is again on an individual, the 'editor', but he is seen as resembling an airline pilot who ought to be in sole charge of his craft but who is buffeted by pressures from customers, crew, airline and weather. In broadcasting the public discussion of freedom tends to focus on the position of the chief executive of the BBC, or of an IBA company, trying to resist outside political pressures. With such varied conceptions of media freedom, an effective policy to protect it is scarcely feasible.

Tunstall, 1983

steady pace, notable in the press. A recent example is the takeover of *The Times* newspaper by Robert Murdoch, who at the time in 1981 already owned the *Sun*, the *News of the World* and many international titles. Meanwhile, within broadcasting, professional independence is such that key decisions concerning their future development have been left to the senior controllers, e.g. the BBC's commitment to compete in local radio with commercial stations, or to participate in satellite broadcasting, despite its resources being stretched. Overall, the Government has an undefined relationship to the media which veers between direct intervention, as in the case of censoring 'video nasties', and indirect pressure, as when it sets the BBC licence fee or the level at which ITV revenue is taxed. The absence of any one single department with responsibility for the media has in practice meant that many vital decisions have been left to the Prime Minister and the Cabinet of the day (this seems to have been the case with allowing Rupert Murdoch to purchase *The Times*).

The uncertainty of to whom the media is accountable has often caused anxiety, not least when it concerns its legal position. One of the most recent of many examples was the decision by the IBA to prevent the screening of a film exposing the excessive degree of surveillance carried out by Britain's security police, MI5 (after considerable public debate, it was eventually decided to allow the film to be screened).

The future: the new technology

The fact that previous policy cycles involving public discussion have lasted on average twelve years may have prompted the current Prime Minister and her Cabinet to eliminate such a debate on the issue of the 'electronic revolution' now taking place. The go-ahead has been given for the rapid expansion of Direct Satellite broadcasting and cable television on the basis that it is economically a 'good thing'. Electronics is a highly competitive international industry, and information technology is seen as the area where there are great profits to be made. Some have questioned whether the huge capital costs involved in developing satellite and cable systems will be recouped, but there is little doubt that these new technologies are here to stay (it is estimated that 70 per cent of US homes will have cable TV by the late 1980s).

The social and political consequences of introducing these new technologies without adequate state control (at present few regulations have been proposed) are hotly disputed. On the one hand, there are those who see cable and satellite broadcasting as offering more choice for the audience, a freer flow of information and opportunities for interactive use (i.e. viewers/listeners being able to communicate with other users as well as the programme source). All of these are seen to pave the way for a more *democratic* society.

On the other hand, critics argue that the new systems will mean that market forces will dominate in a way which will actually lead to less choice and more restricted flow of information. The huge scale of investment in technology associated with cable and satellite broadcasting means that only a few large corporations will be able to participate, and in order to appeal to mass international audiences will produce a 'safe' and predictable diet of entertainment (a mix of soap opera, sport, films, etc.). This means that smaller independent producers will have no outlet, and that 'minority' group interests will be ignored, unlike at present where TV (especially Channel 4 and BBC 2) is committed to serving their needs. This is based on the assumption that public broadcasting as it now exists will be unable effectively to compete with the new satellite and cable channels. These may only be genuine choices for those who are wealthy enough to pay for costly specialist channels, or who can attract advertisers as programme sponsors. Instead of democratic principles, the only governing principle will be profit, and therefore all that is worthwhile about our present public system (for all its shortcomings) will be undermined. The debate continues, but as yet little in the way of a clearly formulated policy towards these issues has emerged.

PART 3

Statistical and documentary readings

Introduction

The readings and tables presented here broadly follow the discussion as it evolves in Part 2 of the book. The extent to which market forces shape media production is raised in the first five readings. These include seeing TV as a form of industrial assembly line (Reading 1), to the influence of advertising (Reading 2 and Fig. 6.2 – these deal with its effect on newspaper choice), to the ratings battle within television (Reading 3) and to the degree of freedom possible for independent production in rock music (Reading 4) and television (Reading 5).

How media represents social reality is the focus of the middle selection of readings and tables. Rather than being a 'window on the world', many sociologists see the media as actively constructing a picture of that world. The creation of moral panics (Reading 6) and the influence of news values (Reading 7) are two of the main themes. The process of news production starts with journalists (Fig. 6.3), but is also determined by powerful social groups (Reading 8). The findings of the Glasgow Media Group lend support to the view of the media as an ideological force in society (Reading 9 and Fig. 6.4). Evaluations of media representations are often made on the basis of either content analysis (Fig. 6.5) or semiological decoding (Readings 10/11).

In the final section are readings and tables related to the role of the audience. Effects research of a psychological (Reading 12) or sociological kind (Reading 13) were dominant until the 1960s when there was a shift to analysing the audience in terms of its uses and gratifications (Fig. 6.6) and the matching of supply and audience demand (Fig. 6.7). The complex nature of media–audience interaction is still very much an open question in media sociology (Reading 14).

In addition to specific questions based on the readings and tables are questions which typify those found on the A level sociology paper (these are listed on pp. 84, 95, 101).

6 Statistics

Figure 6.1 Media consumption

British adults: estimated average hours spent per week with major media, 1982

	Primary activity (narrow definition)	*Primary and secondary activity (looser definition)*	*Primary, secondary and tertiary activity (including set 'switched on', 'looking at' newspaper, etc.)*
Television	18	21	35
Radio	2	23	30
Newspaper and magazines	5	6	10
TOTAL HOURS per week	25	50	75

Source: Tunstall, 1983.

In Fig. 6.1 the three categories of activity are used to try and distinguish the degree of involvement. Thus, under tertiary activity, one might listen to the TV through the wall, awaiting the next programme, or one may even be 'attending' to three media simultaneously! As can be seen, few people listen to the radio without doing something else like driving the car, having a bath, etc.

These figures are becoming harder to produce with any accuracy due to the increased use of video recorders to 'time-switch' viewing, the tendency toward two to three TV sets in one household, and other complicating factors.

The 'Bermuda Triangle' shown in Fig. 6.2 is clearly not related to newspaper circulation, but to its percentage of upper middle class readers (i.e. those defined as AB occupationally; CI refers to

Figure 6.2 The Bermuda Triangle and the death of national newspapers

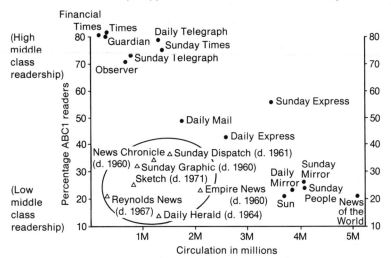

('the last reported position of those national newspapers that have sunk since 1955, as well as the current (1977) plots of the survivors'. Michael Mander)

Note: The seven national newspapers which died between 1960 and 1971 – four of them in 1960–1 – are shown in the circle of lowish circulation and low percentage of ABC1 readers. The survivors were all higher on circulation and/or ABC1 percentage.

Source: Michael Mander. 'The Integration of advertising and circulation sales policies', J. Tunstall, 1983.

routine white collar workers). The most recently established national daily, the *Daily Star*, is very close to the 'triangle', but it has a rising circulation, which seems to make its future secure.

Question

If it were possible for newspapers to be profitable with a relatively small working class readership of between 200–500,000 (as is possible for the 'quality' dailies with an upper middle class readership), how might their content differ from that of the current popular dailies like the *Sun* and the *Mirror*? (NB: new computerised printing technology may reduce costs enough to make this a possibility in the near future.)

Exercise

Construct a social profile of newspapers' 'typical' readers by analysing the advertisements each one carries – jobs, holidays, etc.

Figure 6.3 The news production line

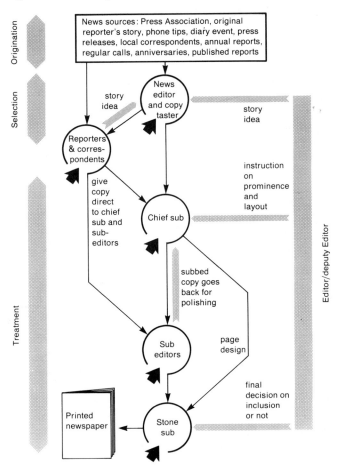

News sources: Press Association, original reporter's story, phone tips, diary event, press releases, local correspondents, annual reports, regular calls, anniversaries, published reports

Origination

Selection

Treatment

Editor/deputy Editor

story idea

News editor and copy taster

story idea

Reporters & correspondents

instruction on prominence and layout

give copy direct to chief sub and sub-editors

Chief sub

subbed copy goes back for polishing

page design

Sub editors

final decision on inclusion or not

Printed newspaper

Stone sub

Point at which story can be altered without knowledge of previous person in chain of production. These alterations can come from the outside, i.e. you.

Source: D. MacShane, 1979.

Fig. 6.3 suggests three stages through which news is produced in newspapers (and to some extent radio and TV): origination, selection and treatment. As can be seen, news does not just happen and then get reported. There are predictable sources, and a clear process of construction through the various *gatekeepers*. Even reporters might not recognise the shape of their original story once it has passed through the editorial stage. Although news is a production line, overall control rests with the editor or deputy editor.

Question

What legal, technical, economic, political and other constraints may influence the production of news within newspapers?

Figure 6.4 The conceptual organisation of industrial news

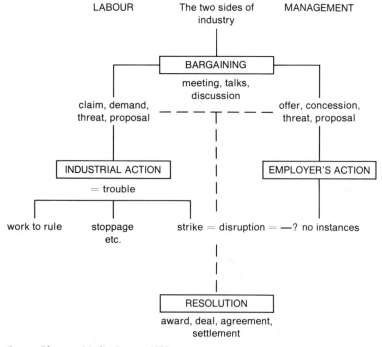

Source: Glasgow Media Group, 1980.

Fig. 6.4 raises the issue of the 'neutrality' of language.

Questions

1 What does Fig. 6.4 suggest about the relative rights of employers and employees?
2 Does this language fit a pluralist view of industrial relations, i.e. a free collective bargaining system in which there is a balance of power between labour and management.
3 What would be the effects if the labels were reversed?
4 What phrase might be used to refer to the action employers and governments take to undermine the effectiveness of workers' industrial action?

Figure 6.5 Television advert content analysis

Five most frequently portrayed occupations on American television according to race and sex

Males Occupation	%	Females Occupation	%
		Blacks	
(N = 95)		(N = 20)	
Govt diplomat	18.9	Nurse	30.0
Musician	13.7	Stage/Dancer	15.0
Policeman	9.5	Musician	5.0
Guard	9.5	Govt diplomat	5.0
Serviceman	5.3	Lawyer	5.0
		Secretary	5.0
Total	56.9	Total	65.0
		British	
(N = 104)		(N = 17)	
Guard	13.5	Nurse	41.2
Musician	11.5	Secretary	11.8
Waiter	7.7	Maid	5.9
Physician	4.8	Govt diplomat	5.9
Serviceman	4.8	Actress	5.9
Total	42.3	Total	70.7
		White Americans	
(N = 1,112)		(N = 260)	
Physician	7.6	Secretary	15.4
Policeman	7.6	Nurse	15.0

Figure 6.5 continued

Five most frequently portrayed occupations on American television according to race and sex

Males Occupation	%	Females Occupation	%
Musician	4.8	Stage/Dancer	8.1
Serviceman	4.6	Maid	6.5
Govt diplomat	4.5	Model	5.0
Total	29.1	Total	50.0

Note: N = actual numbers in sample.

Source: J. Dominick and G. Rauch, 1972.

Questions

1 What does Fig. 6.5 reveal about gender, as represented in adverts on television?
2 Using content analysis, in what other ways could TV representation of gender be investigated?

Exercises

1 Fig. 6.5 refers to fictional American TV in the early 1970s. Try an equivalent analysis of one night's viewing of British TV adverts. You might like to consider other social groups' representation in adverts, like elderly people or teenagers. (This method can equally be applied to other areas of television like soap opera, detective series, etc.)
2 To illustrate a possible shortcoming of content analysis as a method, examine the *variety* of ways in which gender is constructed in adverts. Are some representations undermining or parodying traditional stereotypes?

Figure 6.6 Uses and gratifications of TV quiz programmes

Cluster 1 Self-rating appeal
I can compare myself with the experts
I like to imagine that I am on the programme and doing well
I feel pleased that the side I favour has actually won
I imagine that I was on the programme and doing well
I am reminded of when I was in school
I laugh at the contestant's mistakes
Hard to follow

Cluster 2 Basis for social interaction
I look forward to talking about it with others
I like competing with other people watching with me
I like working together with the family on the answers
I hope the children will get a lot out of it
The children get a lot out of it
It brings the family together sharing the same interest
It is a topic of conversation afterwards
Not really for people like myself

Cluster 3 Excitement appeal
I like the excitement of a close finish
I like to forget my worries for a while
I like trying to guess the winner
Having got the answer right I feel really good
I completely forget my worries
I get involved in the competition
Exciting

Cluster 4 Educational appeal
I find I know more than I thought
I feel I have improved myself
I feel respect for the people on the programme
I think over some of the questions afterwards
Educational

Cluster 5
It is nice to see the experts taken down a peg
It is amusing to see the mistakes some of the contestants make

Cluster 6
I like to learn something as well as to be entertained
I like finding out new things

Cluster 7
I like trying to guess the answers
I hope to find that I know some of the answers

Cluster 8
I find out the gaps in what I know
I learn something new
A waste of time

Cluster 9
Entertaining
Something for all the family

Cluster 10
I like the sound of voices in the house
I like seeing really intelligent contestants showing how much they know

Source: D. McQuail, J. Blumler and J. Brown, 'The television audience: a revised perspective', in McQuail, 1972.

The authors of Fig. 6.6 were trying to discover what kinds of people were most attracted to quiz programmes. A cross section of the population were asked to confirm which of the above statements were closest to their motives for watching quizzes. Particular groups which scored highly for individual clusters were as follows:

1 working class council tenants
2 those with close-knit social networks (extended family, many friends in the neighbourhood)
3 working class viewers who were more than usually isolated
4 those with limited school experience.

Question

What explanations could be offered for these findings regarding social background and TV gratifications?

Exercise

This sort of study could be tried on a variety of programme types of genres. It involves:

1 taping informal conversations about specific programmes with a sample of TV viewers
2 listing the most common motives mentioned for viewing
3 presenting the list to a sample as a self-report study with a graduated response allowed (e.g. from 'very much' to 'slightly' to 'not at all').

Additional questions concerning social background and general attitudes would allow for more complex sociological viewing patterns to be discovered:

4 analysing the resulting data in terms of clusters of statements and correlations with social background.

Figure 6.7 Women's periodicals readership profiles

Women's weekly periodicals readership profiles

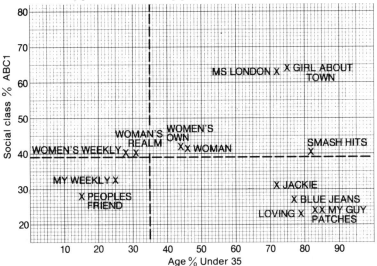

Women's monthly and bi-monthly periodicals

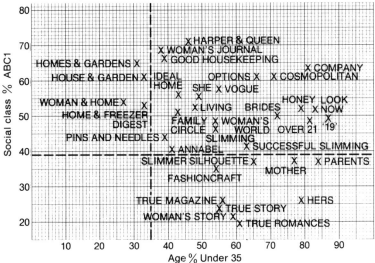

Source: Media World Yearbook, 1983.

Questions

1 In Fig. 6.7 which female groups have the greatest choice of magazine?
2 Which female groups have the least choice of magazine?
3 How far do these profiles support the pluralist case of the media supplying a range of products to meet the varied interests of a heterogenous audience?

(NB: some women's magazines with a small circulation, and which are more difficult to obtain, are excluded from these figures.)

Exercise

Distribute a cross section of women's magazines to the class for a social profile analysis, based on magazine price, style, content, paper quality, adverts, etc. There have been several new magazines published since 1983, which are not therefore covered by these figures. These include *Working Women*, *Just Seventeen*, *Etcetera*, and *Mizz*.

7 Documentary extracts

Reading 1

Now that Britain has four national TV channels, there appears to be a greater choice of programme than ever before. TV would seem to offer a wide scope for creativity and stimulation in both production and viewing. However, in the reading, John Ellis emphasises the standardisation and predictability of TV output, especially through the dominance of the series form. Viewers of soap opera like *Coronation Street* may be surprised at the number of different scriptwriters who have been employed, since the characters and situations never seem to change. Likewise, viewing habits are equally routine. On average, 55 per cent of people who watch an episode of a programme, be it the news, soap opera or a quiz, will watch the next episode.

TV SERIES AS INDUSTRIALISED PRODUCTION

The series form is the basic unit of calculation for TV production, and the basic unit of programme scheduling. Increasingly, all TV broadcast output has been scheduled according to the model of the series: even one-off plays of radically different aesthetic aspirations have been flung together to form a series: *The Wednesday Play*, *Play for Today*, *Second City First*. The series is equally the basic unit of marketing for broadcast TV. Single programmes are not usually advertised (unless special events like a Royal Wedding), but series are. Single episodes can be accounted failures where a series can be a success according to whatever criteria are used. The series is the formal equivalent to industrialised production: it represents the repetition of tasks at the level of programme format, narrative problematic, character and location. The scale of production implied by the series form requires that almost all tasks involved can be performed indiscriminately by anyone of the required grade, except for those acknowledged 'creative' functions which are confined to writer and performer.

Broadcast TV is geared to producing a series commodity consisting of a number (which may be huge, e.g. *Panorama*, news bulletins, etc.) of individual programmes which have a high degree of similarity. The production of these commodities is organised on industrial lines. The tasks involved are specified and personnel are organised into various grades responsible for a particular task or tasks. The tasks involved are standardised as much as possible to provide the maximum interchangeability of labour.

J. Ellis, 1982

Questions

1 Why should marketing and scheduling be so significant for (a) TV controllers; (b) the audience?
2 TV series can normally be categorised into genres, like soap opera. How many distinctive genres exist on TV, and are they scheduled at any particular time? (See p. 18 of Chapter 2 for an explanation of the term 'genre'.)
3 What does Ellis mean when he refers to the 'repetition of tasks at the level of programme format, narrative problematic, character and location'?
4 Is it possible for an individual programme or series to go against convention and undermine or challenge audience expectations?

Exercises (for teacher use)

1 Compile a two to three minute videotape of several extracts from various TV genres, which can then be shown to the class as an identification exercise.
2 To test the extent of genre unity, compile a tape of different examples within a genre, so that the question of how genres evolve can be tackled. For example, the police detective series has passed from *Dixon of Dock Green* to *Z Cars* to *The Sweeney* to *The Bill*, and with it the way police are represented.

Reading 2

Commercial broadcasting as big business is very much the theme of this reading. In America, the profitability of TV companies is primarily based on advertising revenue, which itself depends on the size and make up of the audience for particular programmes. A second source of revenue mentioned is that of programme sales. Within the American system, local TV stations fill most of their airtime with programmes bought from the three national TV corporations.

THE SIGNIFICANCE OF ADVERTISING FOR TELEVISION

In the early days of network broadcasting the production of programmes was the almost exclusive province of advertising agencies. During this period the networks – NBC, CBS and later ABC – contented themselves with profits made from the purchase and resale (to advertisers) of transmission time on groups of stations. But in the 1940s each network began to develop programme packages for commercial sale. This meant increased revenue, which now came from the sale of programmes as well as of time. This development has, of course, led to further concentration of network control: since the network holds an option on the most desirable transmission times on stations coast to coast it will inevitably fill those times with programmes in which it has a financial stake. Indeed the three networks now originate 95 per cent of all programmes transmitted throughout the USA.

Supported by revenues from advertisers, the network is primarily interested in reaching the largest possible number of 'buyers' for the products advertised. The function of the local station is to deliver this audience to the network, which in turn sells it to the advertiser. Various systems – for example, the Nielsen Marketing Research Territory groupings, or Arbitron's Area of Dominant Influence markets – provide potential advertisers with minutely detailed information needed to determine the most efficient way of achieving the desired coverage in specific market areas. In the 'TV market-place' the advertiser 'buys' his viewers at anything between $2\frac{1}{4}$ per thousand 'unassorted' to $10\frac{1}{2}$ a thousand if they can be refined down to particular categories like young women, teenagers and so on, who can be more valuable in that form to sellers of specific products. The sums involved are vast: the average 30-second prime-time network television announcement costs about $60,000 (the highest cost to date, for commercials during the first television broadcast of the film *Gone With the Wind*, was $130,000); even low-rated spots average about $45,000. In 1977, commercial television had total revenues of $5.9 billion and profits of $1.4 billion (*Broadcast Yearbook*, 1979).

M. Gallagher, in M. Gurevitch *et al*., 1982

NB: the rates quoted have since risen to over $500,000 for a 30 second spot during the Superbowl football final (the equivalent of our FA Cup Final).

Questions

1 What effect does advertising have on the programme choice offered to viewers?
2 In America, viewers and listeners in many cities can select from 20–30 TV stations, and 30+ radio stations. Do more stations mean more choice?
3 What difference does the fact that half of British broadcasting is publicly owned make to the sort of output available on TV and radio?

Exercise

By watching the adverts shown on ITV and Channel 4 at different times of the day, try to discover what kind of audience may be watching the programme.

Reading 3

Each week figures are given for the national share of viewers for TV programmes based on monitoring the selections made by a small sample of TV viewers. These are known as the ratings, and are followed with great interest by TV controllers and advertisers. Concern for their showing in the ratings is illustrated in the public debate waged between the BBC and ITV following the publication of the Christmas 1984 viewing figures. ITV claimed 'victory' on the basis of three days viewing (Christmas Eve, Christmas Day and Boxing Day), whilst the BBC claimed 'victory' for the week as a whole. Recently (spring 1985), the

BBC has been making a comeback after a poor year in 1984. Following the introduction of their spring schedules (including a new soap opera, *EastEnders*, a new chat show series hosted by Terry Wogan, and the pushing back of *Panorama* to make way for *Are You Being Served*?), the BBC's overall share of the audience rose from 33 per cent to 45 per cent in just four weeks.

THE RATINGS FOR THE WEEK ENDING 3 MARCH 1985

		Channel	*Co/Country*	*Day*	*Time*	*Type*	*000s*	*TVR*
1	Coronation Street	ITV	GRA	Mon	19.30	Soap	18037	35
2	Last/Summer Wine	BBC1	BBC	Sun	20.10	Lt Ent	16748	33
3	Coronation Street	ITV	GRA	Wed	19.29	Soap	16552	32
4	Ms Marple: Mdr/Acd	BBC1	BBC	Fri	21.30	Film	15357	30
5	Only Fools/Horses	BBC1	BBC	Thu	19.59	D/S	14886	29
6	Weekend News/Wthr	BBC1	BBC	Fri	21.26	News	14677	29
7	Ms Marple: Mdr/Acd	BBC1	BBC	Sat	21.14	Film	14473	28
8	One By One	BBC1	BBC	Sat	19.19	Lt Ent	14271	28
9	EastEnders	BBC1	BBC	Tue	–	Soap	14196	27
10	Busman's Holiday	ITV	GRA	Tue	19.29	Quiz	14142	27
11	Odd One Out	BBC1	BBC	Fri	19.42	Lt Ent	14077	27
12	Game For/Laugh	ITV	LWT	Sun	19.15	Lt Ent	14004	27
13	Are/Being Served?	BBC1	BBC	Mon	20.29	D/S	13834	27
14	Ms Marple: Mdr/Acd	BBC1	BBC	Thu	21.31	Film	13762	27
15	Cover Her Face	ITV	ANG	Sun	20.45	D/S	13743	27
16	This Is Your Life	ITV	THA	Wed	20.00	Lt Ent	13641	27
17	Roll Over Beethoven	ITV	CEN	Mon	20.01	Comedy	13620	26
18	That's Life	BBC1	BBC	Sun	21.54	Mag	13594	26
19	Quincy	ITV	U.S.	Mon	21.04	D/S	13476	26
20	Wish You Were Here	ITV	THA	Wed	19.00	Mag	13448	26
21	Starsky And Hutch	BBC1	U.S.	Fri	20.12	D/S	13440	26
22	News And Sport	BBC1	BBC	Sat	20.55	Sport	13375	26
23	Emmerdale Farm	ITV	YTV	Tue	–	Soap	13226	25
24	9 O'Clock News	BBC1	BBC	Fri	21.00	News	13092	25
25	Dynasty	BBC1	U.S.	Sat	20.09	Soap	12935	25
26	The Price is Right	ITV	CEN	Sat	–	Quiz	12573	25
27	EastEnders	BBC1	BBC	Thu	–	Soap	12613	24
28	Fresh Fields	ITV	THA	Tue	20.31	Sit Com	12515	24
29	All Star Secrets	ITV	LWT	Sat	19.19	Lt Ent	12507	24
30	Me And My Girl	ITV	LWT	Fri	19.00	D/S	12129	24
31	News/Weather	BBC1	BBC	Sun	21.10	News	12084	23
32	Up Elephant/Castle	ITV	THA	Tue	20.00	Lt Ent	11687	23

THE RATINGS FOR THE WEEK ENDING 3 MARCH 1985

	Channel	Co/Country	Day	Time	Type	000s	TVR
33 T J Hooker	ITV	U.S.	Sat	–	D/S	11543	22
34 The Practice	ITV	GRA	Sun	20.16	D/S	10940	21
35 The Practice	ITV	GRA	Fri	19.30	D/S	10925	21
36 For/Few Dollars More	BBC1	U.S.	Mon	22.07	Film	10883	21
37 What's My Line	ITV	THA	Mon	19.01	Quiz	10740	21
38 Mastermind	BBC1	BBC	Sun	20.41	Quiz	10735	21
39 9 O'Clock News	BBC1	BBC	Tue	21.00	News	10550	21
40 Wogan	BBC1	BBC	Fri	19.00	Mag	10516	20
41 Top Of The Pops	BBC1	BBC	Thu	19.30	Music	10085	20
42 Question Of Sport	BBC1	BBC	Thu	20.30	Sport	10085	20
43 Aspel And Company	ITV	LWT	Sat	22.04	Mag	10071	20
44 Maelstrom	BBC1	BBC	Tue	20.05	D/S	10054	20
45 Wogan	BBC1	BBC	Mon	19.00	Mag	9917	19
46 News At Ten	ITV	ITN	Mon	22.00	News	9882	19
47 Blankety Blank	BBC1	BBC	Tue	19.30	Quiz	9777	19
48 World Cup Special	BBC1	BBC	Wed	19.26	Sport	9672	19
49 Miami Vice	BBC1	U.S.	Tue	21.28	D/S	9657	19
50 There Comes/Time	ITV	YTV	Wed	20.31	Comedy	9509	19

Broadcast, 1985.

Questions

1 Much has been made of the tendency of viewers to stay with one channel all evening, or for a programme which follows a very popular one to inherit its audience. Do the above ratings lend support to this argument for any particular evening on either the BBC or ITV?
2 What effect might the growing use of video tapes for 'times-witching' of programmes have on the validity of the ratings figures (or even on advertisers given the ability of video users to fast forward through adverts)?

Exercise in scheduling (for teachers)

Give the class a random list of TV programmes together with their running length (the top 100 is published in *Broadcast*), and ask groups of students to compile an evening's viewing between 6.30 and 10.00 pm to try and achieve a maximum ratings.

Reading 4

Whilst no media output is guaranteed audience popularity, some parts are more uncertain than others. Prominent examples are the publishing and music industries. However, low unit production costs enable more risks to be taken, and failures to be written off against a few large successes. It also means that the large companies cannot control the market so easily. Within rock music, new tastes and styles often develop locally at street level and then get noticed by the music business. This, it is argued below, leads to a cyclical pattern whereby there is always space for innovation from 'below', and even a rejection of commercially 'safe' products – a case of 'no more heroes' according to the punk movement.

ROCK MUSIC MARKET CYCLES

As we have noted record companies tend to focus on styles which sell reliably and exploit the existing roster of artists. Once they have identified a successful sound and market they tend to devote considerable resources to promoting this area at the expense of the others. At the same time, inevitably, styles, tastes and preferences change so most record companies eventually have to investigate new areas. Some do this with enthusiasm: most are less than willing, and once having shifted are wont to try to consolidate once again.

Peterson and Berger have argued that this approach leads to a *cyclic* phenomenon. Original ideas and styles, generated more or less spontaneously, are then taken up (after some resistance, hesitation and modification) by the industry, which then clings on to them. Meanwhile new creative trends emerge which have to break through the new 'monopoly'. Thus a cycle of innovation and consolidation develops. According to Berger and Peterson, this cycle is also reflected in the pattern of 'economic concentration' and market control. Monopolistic conglomerates are formed during boom periods, based on a certain confluence of styles, and inhibit the growth of independents – who are usually the only source of new ideas. There then follows a sudden burst of innovation and economic dis-aggregation – with new small record labels emerging, to pioneer the new sound and style, followed once again by a re-concentration and stagnation as the majors gain control . . .

Peterson and Berger argue that the trends in market share can be inversely correlated with both musical innovation and consumer satisfaction: that is to say that during the periods when the majors dominated (e.g. 1948–55), innovation was stifled and there was unsatiated consumer demand for new types of music as opposed to the bland offerings of the majors. Pressure thus built up for innovation (rock and roll) and once released this led to a rapid re-ordering of market shares, with monopoly replaced by competition.

A comparative lull in innovation then followed, with the majors' market shares gradually increasing until the next major innovation – the arrival of the Beatles, followed by the west coast hippy rock music of the late 1960s. The boom in sales left plenty of room for everyone, although in this final period (1970–3) the majors gradually re-established dominance and (arguably) innovation decreased. Events since then (i.e. after 1973) initially tended to confirm Peterson and Berger's prognosis – that re-concentration would lead to a new period of ossification and lack of innovation. It was not until 1976 that a new wave of groups and independent labels emerged to undermine the majors' monopoly. Whether the *whole* cycle will be repeated – with the majors successfully absorbing the new wave and/or otherwise re-establishing market control – is however far from clear.

D. Elliott, 1982

It could be that the current importance of music videos as promotional material with high production values (and hence costs) has placed the large record companies firmly in control.

Questions

1 How justified is the distinction between a spontaneous, creative and authentic 'street' youth culture and a commercially 'manufactured' youth culture?
2 Does one have priority or dominance over the other?
3 Is it inevitable that once appropriated by large corporations, rock music is defused of any 'resistance' or subcultural meaning?

Reading 5

TV appears to many to be an exciting, glamorous and creative medium within which to work. However, as we saw in Reading 1, the reality may be rather different. Media organisations may not be unlike business or administrative organisations, i.e. having a clearly defined hierarchical division of labour, in which there is little room for individual deviation. The reading contains the observations of Stuart Hood, ex Controller of BBC programmes.

OCCUPATIONAL SOCIALISATION

What is common to both BBC and the commercial television companies, however, is the process of learning the rules of the institution, which begins as soon as anyone is appointed to their staff. This process is mainly an informal one and is at work in any large organisation. It is true that in the case of the BBC there are in-house training courses, which are a formal part of the process of moulding staff so that they will function well and efficiently within the limits set by the organisation; but as in other organisations much of what the newcomers learn is picked up from colleagues at work, in the canteen or in the pub favoured by their associates. They may learn that a story or programme idea which they consider 'interesting' is not so, that certain people are not suitable subjects for interview, or that certain words to describe persons or events are 'inappropriate', that a particular piece of film is not suitable for inclusion in a programme or only in certain circumstances or in certain contexts . . .

To information acquired in the day-to-day contacts of work and leisure must be added the contents of the directives which filter down through large organisations from policy meetings. These are gatherings of senior executives at which gate-keeping in the grand manner goes on, where – in the news departments, for instance – decisions are taken as to which events should be covered by film or television cameras, where it is laid down what names should be applied to groups or individuals and who shall be allowed access to the microphone or television camera. Membership of such policy-making committees is restricted but there are departmental meetings at which the directives emanating from the policy-

makers are passed on, discussed and interpreted. By partici-
pating at meetings at departmental level newcomers learn
how the organisation works, what policies it pursues, what
degree of latitude is possible within the bounds of policy.
They learn here and by experience in what directions the
organisation is prepared to be liberal and what directions it is
not. They will become aware over a period of time of changes
in policy and discover that within the organisation there are
different tendencies, for even an organisation like the BBC is
not monolithic; it can accommodate what are seen – in
organisational terms – as progressives and conservatives . . .

But above all they must learn the limits of the possible – the
limits set by the management of the BBC, by the management
of the television companies and by their supervisory body, the
Independent Broadcasting Authority.

Hood, 1980

Questions

1 Does this account fit a view of TV organisations as well
   ordered, predictable and rather rigid structures (a Weberian
   view), or as open to negotiation and change (an interactionist
   view)?
2 What may be the 'limits of the possible' within television?
3 Are there any recent examples of these limits being stretched
   or negotiated in particular programmes or series?

Essay question relating to Chapter 2

Examine the relationship between ownership, control and production within the media.

Reading 6

Stan Cohen's text *Folk Devils and Moral Panics* is a post-war British
sociological classic. By observing the events, interviewing the
participants and checking offical data like court records, Cohen
was able to show the extent to which the media *socially constructed*
a moral panic. He singled out three specific types of distortion
involved as described below. Readers might like to draw parallels
with more recent moral panics like soccer hooliganism.

THE MEDIA AND MORAL PANICS

Exaggeration and Distortion:
The major type of distortion in the inventory lay in exaggerating grossly the seriousness of the events, in terms of criteria such as the number taking part, the number involved in violence and the amount and effects of any damage or violence. Such distortion took place primarily in terms of the mode and style of presentation characteristic of most crime reporting; the sensational headlines, the melodramatic vocabulary and the deliberate heightening of those elements in the story considered as news. The regular use of phrases such as 'riot', 'orgy of destruction', 'battle', 'attack', 'siege', 'beat up the town' and 'screaming mob' left an image of a besieged town from which innocent holidaymakers were fleeing to escape a marauding mob . . .

Prediction:
. . . This is the implicit assumption, present in virtually every report, that what had happened was inevitably going to happen again. Few assumed that the events were transient occurrences; the only questions were where the Mods and Rockers would strike next and what could be done about it. As will be suggested, these predictions played the role of the classical self-fulfilling prophecy. Unlike the case of natural disasters where the absence of predictions can be disastrous, with social phenomena such as deviance, it is the presence of predictions that can be 'disastrous'.

The predictions in the inventory period took the form of reported statements from local figures such as tradesmen, councillors and police spokesmen about what should be done 'next time' or of immediate precautions they had taken. More important, youths were asked in TV interviews about their plans for the next Bank Holiday and interviews were printed with either a Mod or Rocker theatening revenge 'next time' . . .

Symbolization:
Communication, and especially the mass communication of stereotypes, depends on the symbolic power of words and images. Neutral words such as place-names can be made to symbolize complex ideas and emotions; for example, Pearl Harbor, Hiroshima, Dallas and Aberfan. A similar process

occurred in the Mods and Rockers inventory: these words themselves and a word such as 'Clacton' acquired symbolic powers. It became meaningful to say 'we don't want another Clacton here' or 'you can see he's one of those Mod types'.

S. Cohen, 1972

Questions

1 To what extent is the media acting alone in the creation of such a moral panic?
2 Whose views, and what possible explanations, are absent in media accounts of such events?

Exercise

Cohen refers to the symbolic power of words and images:
1 Try to compile lists of such symbolisation within media coverage of other social groups/events, e.g. industrial relations.
2 From newspaper photos and TV film and video footage, examine how words transform the symbolic meaning of the images (this might be done by removing the newspaper caption and film commentary, and asking the class to provide the words).

Reading 7

News values refer to the informal, and usually unstated, assumptions which underlie journalists' reasons for selecting stories as being newsworthy, i.e. to be given priority. Below is a list of the most significant news values. They don't exhaust all the possibilities, and obviously the 'best' stories combine several of them at once.

NEWS VALUES

1. *Frequency* The time-span taken by an event. Murders take very little time and their meaning is quickly arrived at. Hence their frequency fits that of daily newspapers and programmes. On the other hand, economic, social or cultural trends take very much longer to unfold and to be made meaningful: they

are outside the frequency of daily papers. Thus they have to be 'marked' (if they are reported at all) by means of devices like the release of reports or statistics on a particular day.

2. *Threshold* The size of an event. There is a threshold below which an event will not be reported at all (varying in intensity between, for instance, local and national news). And once reported, there is a further threshold of drama: the bigger the story, the more added drama is needed to keep it going. War reporting is an example of this. Already very big news, its coverage is unlikely to increase unless an especially cataclysmic event happens.

3. *Unambiguity* The clarity of an event. Events don't have to be simple, necessarily (though that helps), but the range of possible meanings must be limited . . .

4. *Meaningfulness* (a) Cultural proximity: events that accord with the cultural background of the news-gatherers will be seen as more meaningful than others, and so more liable to be selected . . . (b) Relevance: events in far-off cultures, classes or regions will nevertheless be newsworthy if they impinge on the news-gatherer's 'home' culture – usually in the form of a threat; as with OPEC and the (mostly Arab) countries with oil – their lifestyles, customs and beliefs are suddenly fascinating for Western journalists.

5. *Consonance* The predictability of, or desire for, an event. If the media expect something to happen, then it will . . .

6. *Unexpectedness* The unpredictability, or rarity, of an event. Of course it is within the *meaningful* (4) and the *consonant* (5) that the unexpected is to be found. Hence the 'newness' of unexpected events usually gets discovered in thoroughly familiar, expected contexts.

7. *Continuity* The 'running story'. If an event is covered, it will continue to be covered for some time.

8. *Composition* The mixture of different kinds of event. If a newspaper or TV bulletin is packed with major foreign stories, a relatively insignificant domestic story will be included to balance the mixture. Alternatively, if a major story is running, other similar events may be selected for inclusion in a 'round-up' of stories on that subject . . .

9. *Reference to elite nations* Stories about wars, elections and disasters are good examples of this tendency. Wars involving the USA, USSR, or forces explicitly allied to one or the other, will be reported, whereas others go virtually unnoticed . . . Elections in France, Germany and Italy will receive more coverage than those in Latin America, Africa, etc. And of course there is the famous head–count equation for disasters: disasters in Bangladesh, for example, need thousands or hundreds killed to reach the newsworthiness threshold, whereas those in 'elite' countries will be newsworthy with progressively lower body–counts.

10. *Reference to elite persons* Firstly because it is assumed their actions are more consequential than the daily activities of ordinary people – they 'affect our lives'. Secondly, the social activities of elite people can serve as representative actions – their weddings, opinions, nights out and domestic habits are taken to be of interest to us all, since we too engage in these things . . .

11. *Personalisation* Events are seen as the actions of people as individuals. Individual people are easier to identify – and to identify with – than structures, forces or institutions: hence 'the government' is often personalised as 'Mrs Thatcher', etc.

12. *Negativity* Bad news is good news. It is generally *unexpected* (6), *unambiguous* (3), it *happens quickly* (1), it is *consonant* (5) with general expectations about the state of the world, and hence its *threshold* (2) is lower than that for positive news.

J. Hartley, 1982

Questions

1 What kind of picture of social reality is likely to be produced through the application of these news values?
2 How might the reporting of the following be shaped by news values: (a) industrial relations; (b) race relations?

Exercises

1 What news values are reflected in these two front pages of the *Times* and the *Sun* newspapers?

THE TIMES

No 62,073　　　WEDNESDAY FEBRUARY 27 1985　　　(23p)

THE TIMES
1785-1985

Tomorrow

Out of this world
Profile of science fiction
writer Arthur C Clarke

Israel's Vietnam
A Christopher Walker finds
opinion split on the
Lebanese withdrawal

Solzhenitsyn
I count Nikolai Tolstoy
reviews Michael
Scammell's biography

Mental gymnastics
I Enter the soccer
pools, helping to deal
with sporting stress

Portfolio

The Time Portfolio competition
daily prize of £2,000 was
shared by two winners yesterday. Miss Victoria Bourne of
Southampton, Hampshire and
Mr C Dedman of Wolver-
ness, Essex, each received
£1,000. Portfolio list, page 22;
how to play, information
service, back page.
On Saturday £72,000 is available to be won — the £20,000
weekly prize, as well as the
daily prize of £2,000.

Porn videos turned 'Fox' into rapist

Pornographic videos turned
Malcolm Fairley, a labourer,
from a small-time thief into the
rapist known as the Fox, a judge
said yesterday. Mrs Jill Knight,
Conservative MP for Edgbas-
ton, demanded a government
clampdown on pornography
after Fairley was given six life
sentences. **Page 3**

Mafia roundup

Nine leaders of New York's five
organised crime families were
arrested and accused by a
federal grand jury of ordering
executions and supervising mob
operations. **Page 6**

Princely concern

The Prince of Wales told the
Institute of Directors that
Britain's shattered communities
could not be healthy of finance
alone but by letting people hold
sway. **Page 10**

THE TIMES

Win a 1985 BMW
for a 1935 price. **Page 8**

Pretoria relents

South Africa conceded that the
Crossroads black squatter settle-
ment outside Cape Town could
become a permanent township.
Pretoria news curbs, page 6

Interpol chief

A Scotland Yard Special Branch
officer, Mr Raymond Kendall,
has taken over as acting
secretary-general of Interpol
Page 7

SPECIAL REPORT

One hundred years of notable
achievement is celebrated this
week in City and Guilds,
could not be healthy of Imperial
College, London. A five-page
report looks at how tomorrow's
engineers are being taught to
become permanent. Pages 15-21

England lose

England look unlikely to qualify
for the semi-finals of the world
championship of cricket in
Australia after losing to India
John Woodcock, page 26

Leader page, 11
Letters: On arts row, from Mr
S Warsy; Sir Thomas
Boardman and Dr H Harris
Leading articles: The BBC, Mr
Lange's visit; Drug campaign
Features, pages 8-10
Minterrand's New Caledonian
predicament: Philip Howard
on democracy's end enemies
Spectrum: Charlie Chaplin and
the PR
Obituary, page 12
Mr Douglas Muggeridge; Mr
Efrem Zimbalist

Miners' strike near to collapse in militant areas

● The national executive of the NUM
has been called into session in Sheffield
tomorrow as hard line supporters of the
strike were privately predicting a "a final
back to work".

● Another 1,464 miners went back to
work yesterday, bringing the total for the
two days to 9,308 and making 93,000
NUM members not now on strike.

● Rail staff are to be told by British Rail
to ignore union instructions banning coal
movement or risk the threat of no more than
2,000 jobs.

● 14 lawful assembly charges against 21
South Yorkshire miners amid charges of
damaging property and threatening behaviour were formally dismissed by Notting-
ham magistrates yesterday.

By Paul Routledge, Labour Editor

BR to deliver 'jobs or freight' warning

By David Felton, Labour Correspondent

Mass arrest 'a picket line policy'

By Craig James

FAIR FOR TEACHERS

Mrs Kinnock, displaying a NUT poster, at the start of the teachers' strike (Photograph: Barry Beattie)

2,000 schools close in teachers' strike

By Lucy Hodges, Education Correspondent

Foot attack on former Speaker

By Anthony Bevins
Political Correspondent

Pound recovers after $1.037 low

By David Smith, Energy Correspondent

63 per cent of parents favour school caning

Zia delighted with 53% turn-out

From Michael Hamlyn
Islamabad

Civil servants 'duty is to ministers'

By Julian Haviland,
Political Editor

Nitze is hopeful on Star Wars

From Nicholas Ashford
Washington

Continued on back page, col 3

FACE OF EVIL . . . Malcolm Fairley put thousands in fear as The Fox

THE Sun

Wednesday, February 27, 1985   18p   TODAY'S TV: PAGE 12

'You desecrated and defiled men and women, old and youthful' MR JUSTICE CAULFIELD YESTERDAY

PORN LUST OF THE FOX

Beast gets six life sentences

By IAN HEPBURN and TONY SNOW

THE BRUTAL rapist dubbed The Fox was given SIX life sentences yesterday for his sickening crimes.

Malcolm Fairley, 32, based his lustful attacks on hard-core porn videos hired from sex shops.

He believed "victims" in the sordid films enjoyed what was being done to them. And as Fairley, an illiterate labourer, was sentenced at St Albans Crown Court, the judge Mr Justice Caulfield told him:

⬤ You have desecrated and defiled men and women, old and youthful in their own homes which you then pillaged.

I am satisfied that you are a decadent advertisement for the evil pornographers. They will want to forget you as one of their worst casualties. ⬤

Fairley, of Kentish Town, North London, received the M A X I M U M sentence on each of the 13 charges.

LIFE for three rapes and on three charges of burglary with intent to rape.

14 YEARS on each of five counts of burglary and entering homes with *Continued on Page Five*

FULL AMAZING STORY—See Pages 4, 5, 15, 16, 17 and 18

2 *Choosing the news* – a simulation where groups of students prepare a 10–15 minute news bulletin (for recording on audio or video tape) from a stream of stories supplied by the teacher (copied from a day's newspaper/TV news items of an earlier date – or it may be possible to supply video footage from the TV news). Afterwards, the students' criteria for selecting, editing and ordering stories is evaluated in class.

Reading 8

As part of their work on the law and order 'crisis' generated in the 1970s, the CCCS authors of *Policing the Crisis* used the case of mugging to show how the media helped create a moral panic. Although there was no such official crime, and there was little reason for the scale of the concern expressed at the time, it was made to appear as if our streets were suddenly full of muggers preying on vulnerable and innocent members of the public. In the extract below, Stuart Hall raises the issue of who has the power to gain access to the media and define the nature of criminal behaviour like mugging.

MUGGING

So the media do not act on their own. Of course, crime is always news, and some papers keep a constant watch on this tantalising topic of crime. But the media also depend on the definers of crime – the police, the courts, the Home Secretary – to identify the main movements in the incidence of crime, so that when you get headlines in the press about crime waves, those headlines depend on the institutional links between those who define and control crime and those who report it as news . . .

The police draw attention to the rise in 'muggings' and the judges comment on that rise when they are delivering sentences, and the media report both. They form a sort of circle with the other institutions that are involved, and the 'mugging' topic then gets transferred from the courts and the police to the media. At the same time, the way that these other institutional spokesmen, the police and the courts, see the crime becomes the primary definition of 'mugging' in the press . . .

Each aspect of the public debate about 'mugging' passes through the media. They form the link between the definers and controllers, the public and the news.

Now, of course, the media don't express personal opinions about events . . . Television is required by the charters to be objective and impartial. Even in the press, where editorial opinions do get expressed, a distinction is drawn between opinion and fact. But this requirement to be 'objective' means that the media must rely heavily on the official definers. The television reporter, for example, substantiates everything he says by referring to what the definers have said, by quoting an authority, and some definers always get quoted: they have a right to be heard. Powerful opinions stand highest in the pyramid of access to the media, and this means that the media naturally incline towards, and tend to reproduce, the definitions of those people who are powerful in the society. The media pick up their definitions first. It is they who define the topic.

You may think that doesn't matter, but there are always alternative points of view, alternative explanations for events. There are few actions, however awful, which are meaningless or absolutely without motive or cause for those people who do them. Accounts which do not fit neatly with the primary definitions do, of course, sometimes also get access to the media. But they do not have access as of right – these opinions come later.

Stuart Hall, in *The Listener*, 1 May 1975

Questions

1 What is the media's role within the spiral of concern generated over mugging (often referred to as an 'amplification spiral')?
2 In what way does this account go beyond the usual interactionist version of the labelling process?
3 What space exists within the media for alternative definitions of reality?

Reading 9

This reading is a brief summary of what the Glasgow Media Group see as the main explanation for the partial and restricted view which is presented within TV news (rather than an impartial and 'balanced' view). By *inferential framework* they mean the unspoken assumptions which underlie the reporting, e.g. stories which relate to the economic system always accept its legitimacy and normalcy.

THE JOURNALISTS' WORLD VIEW

In the period of our study, the news was organised and produced substantially around the views of the dominant political group in our society. We have shown how the views of those who disagree fundamentally with this position, or who offered alternative approaches, were downgraded and underrepresented in the news coverage. This is in stark comparison with the careful explanation and heavy emphasis given to the dominant analysis and the political policies which flowed from it . . .

. . . Our argument, then, is that the world view of journalists will prestructure what is taken to be important or significant. It will do this in two ways. First it will affect the character and content of specific inferential frames used in the news, as we showed above in relation to the definition of what industrial problems are. Second, it will set general boundaries on where news is looked for, and on who are the significant individuals the 'important' people to be interviewed, etc.

Glasgow Media Group, 1980

Questions

1 Which 'dominant group' are the authors referring to?
2 With reference to Fig. 6.4 what are the inferential frames regarding solutions to the economic crisis, and the issue of industrial conflict?

Reading 10

DECODING NEWS TITLES

Title sequences are a rich source of images and sounds for a semiological reading. Apart from signalling the start of a new programme, they represent what ideas, meanings and pleasures are about to be made available to viewers. Very often, programmes belonging to a particular genre carry similar sorts of coding within the titles. News programmes are a typical example.

BBC: 9 o'clock news
1 *Music/voiceover*
Steady guitar rhythm → announcement of the news → three ascending musical climaxes drums/trumpet fanfare → final musical climax with cymbals

Connotation
The music suggests urgency, technical immediacy and imminent drama

2 *Image*	*Connotation*
(a) Blacked out newsdesk with a backdrop satellite shot of Britain	We await the spotlight on tonight's 'star' newsreaders; plus a technically privileged (objective?) perspective of Britain
(b) Streams of yellow squares flow into London	News is being assembled from all corners of the globe; London is the news capital (of the world?)
(c) Blue streaks flow out of London to form the 9 o'clock news title as it rotates into view above Britain	The news logo and accompanying graphics and music resembles the titles of a Hollywood space adventure

News titles, like the *9 o'clock news*, tend to signify (a) a sense of immediacy, urgency and drama, and (b) an imposing of order and structure on disorder and chaos, i.e. the events out there in the world.

An examination of other news programme titles would reveal variations on these themes, e.g. the *News at 10* Big Ben chimes, or the coalescing of global maps in *Newsnight* on BBC2.

Exercise

This kind of analysis can be attempted on virtually any TV titles, but is best done within genres like soap opera or police detectives.

Reading 11

DECODING ADVERTS

Adverts generally aim to promote sales of a product. Given a market where consumers do not have unlimited resources, and where many products are similar in price and function, the goal of adverts is to make the product more desirable by adding to it some extra quality not obviously present. Outrageous or misleading claims are generally prevented by the Advertising Standards Authority (ASA), thus suggestions have to be implicit, i.e. coded through the signs which make up an advert. These codes are ideological in the sense that they convey qualities and make connections which appear to be natural but are in fact contrived.

Exercise

1 Select adverts for groups of similar products like perfume, alcohol or cigarettes, and analyse how the 'signs' within the adverts convey feelings or qualities that are supposed to be realised through purchase and consumption.
2 Compile a selection of TV adverts for classroom decoding. The main sign systems present are: (i) images; (ii) music; (iii) the spoken word. These are interrelated to form meaning, but can be isolated through (a) turning the sound off, and asking the class to write a script for the characters and voice over; or (b) turning the vision off, and asking the class to construct the images. (Obviously, this will work more effectively with the less well-known adverts.)

Essay questions relating to Chapter 3

1 'The media don't simply mirror social reality, they actively help to construct it for us.' Discuss, with reference to such social areas as industrial relations, politics and deviance.
2 Examine the view that the main role of the media is one of social control.

Reading 12

In this reading, the authors contrast the work of Dr Belson, mainly behaviourist psychology, i.e. a search for a cause which stimulates or conditions a given behavioural response, with that of ethnographic sociology, an attempt to understand the meaning of behaviour by observing people in their natural social setting. The 'TV as the cause of violence view' is attractive to those looking for a scapegoat for complex social problems.

A recent example was the claim that the 1981 summer riots were mainly due to teenagers imitating what they had seen on TV. However, subsequent research showed that few of the teenagers involved had followed the events on TV. Indeed, there was found to be a strong anti-media feeling among them. Instead, the troubles were seen to be more related to the tension which existed between bored young male, and often black, teenagers and aggressive, and often racist, policing policies.

VIEWS FROM THE BOYS: ETHNOGRAPHIC PERSPECTIVES

Dr Belson is not alone in concentrating on teenage boys. They have also been the main focus of most of the ethnographic studies of delinquency. The past couple of years or so have produced several notable contributions to this genre, including Howard Parker and Owen Gill on Liverpool, Paul Willis on Wolverhampton, and Dave Robins and Phil Cohen on the East End. Although they cover some of the same ground as Belson, they approach it very differently. Where Belson opts for a large cross-sectional sample from all over London, they opt for intensive studies of particular groups of working-class boys in specific localities. Where Belson uses interviews and self-report schedules, they rely on observations of actual behaviour coupled with repeated conversations and informal interviews over a period of months, sometimes years. Where Belson aims to establish a link between high exposure to violent television programmes and high involvement in acts of violence, they set out to explore the ways in which acts of violence and other forms of delinquency arise out of specific social situations and sets of relations, and are underpinned by particular meanings drawn from wider class and neighbourhood cultures . . .

The ethnographic evidence points to a strong connection between involvement in violence (particularly vandalism and fighting) and immersion in the male street culture rooted in the working-class neighbourhood. It also indicates that the impact of televised violence is relatively marginal. This does not mean that television has no impact, but it does suggest (1) that it is a subsidiary factor and (2) that its effects are mediated through the pre-existing situational cultures.

G. Murdoch and R. McCron,
The Broadcasting and Delinquency Debate,
Screen Education, Spring 1979

Questions

1 What are the suggested shortcomings of Belson's research approach?
2 What strengths are claimed for the ethnographic method?
3 How might the meaning of TV violence for working class boys on the street differ from other social groups?

Reading 13

From 1940 till the mid 1960s, there were about a dozen major studies of the media's effect on voters during election campaigns, most of which adopted the panel sample method pioneered in the *People's Choice*. As a result of these studies, two myths were demolished: first of an all-powerful media moulding the public's political thinking, and secondly of the rational voter, trying to decide which party has the best policies before going out and voting.

THE MEDIA AND THE VOTERS: A SUMMARY OF EFFECTS
RESEARCH

1. Despite the many differences among countries and from election to election, typically about 80 per cent, or more, of the voters have made up their minds about their vote before the campaign begins, that is at least several months prior to the election . . .
2. The changers – those who shift from one party to another *during* the campaign – have been found to be relatively uninterested in the election and its outcome. The voter with a high interest in politics is much more likely to have made up his mind early, and to hold firmly to his intention throughout the campaign . . .
3. It follows from the fact that the changers are recruited from among those least interested in politics that they are not much exposed to mass communications about politics . . .
4. Election broadcasting is often kinder to the opposition party and to the newcomer. Blumler and McQuail argue that the persistence of a third party in England may have been given a boost by television,

'partly because of its high popularity and the heavy use made of it by the more vulnerable viewers, partly because the Liberals received a relatively generous share of TV time, and partly because of the sheltered status that politics enjoys in the programme schedules of British broadcasting . . .'

5. There seems to be an underlying party loyalty on the part of most people in countries with reasonably stable political systems . . .

6. The combination of a low degree of loyalty and yet some exposure to election communications has become a more probable combination in the era of television than ever before. Large numbers of people are watching election broadcasts not because they are interested in politics but because they like viewing television . . .

7. More than the mass media are able to convert, they reinforce vote intentions and the basic loyalties underlying them . . . Those who are 'seeking reinforcement' are more politically interested, and more politically sophisticated. They are more selective in their viewing, and are often looking for ammunition for political arguments with others. They use the media to help adjust their political attitudes to those articulated by their party.

8. Sometimes, as certain studies show, the media influence votes indirectly by focusing on an issue which, in turn, affects the frame of reference of the 'guidance seekers', and perhaps others . . .

9. The mass media rarely work alone, whether to reinforce or convert. The mass media, rather, stimulate discussion, and the discussion clinches – or negates – the effect . . .

10. In explaining the attention paid by voters to the election campaign, and it is considerable, there are even more important motives at work than the manifestly political ones of 'guidance seeking' and 'reinforcement seeking' . . . People expose themselves to party propaganda, and to election communications, because they want to know 'what will happen' to them and/or to their country. They want to see what their leaders look like. Blumler and McQuail call these functions 'surveillance'.

E. Katz, 'Platforms and windows:
broadcasting's role in Election Campaigns',
in McQuail, 1972

Questions

1 What does Katz mean when he distinguishes between 'guidance seeking' and 'reinforcement seeking' motives of voters?
2 Why should TV's commitment to impartiality and 'balance' favour a third party in British politics (point 4)? (NB: this was published in 1972, when the Liberals only had 10–15 per cent vote. Currently, the Liberal/SDP Alliance has between 20–5 per cent support. Perhaps this might lead to a more critical treatment by TV.)
3 With which specific issues might the media influence voters by 'affecting the frame of reference of the "guidance seekers"' (point 8)?
4 Why might point 6 have been undervalued by the researchers?

Reading 14

In this extract, Hartmann and Husband summarise the findings of their research into the media's role in affecting attitudes towards race. The main contrast they make is between situationally based knowledge, i.e. derived from first hand experience of living in an area with a large black population, and media relayed knowledge, i.e. second hand knowledge. Of course, in reality these are ideal types, since there is an interaction between the two – local situational beliefs get reported by the media, and, in turn, the media's coverage may help to shape interpretations and understandings of the local situation.

THE MEDIA AND ATTITUDES TOWARDS RACE

What then is the nature of the media contribution? We might approach this by comparing the type of response most closely associated with the media with the type of response most commonly associated with personal experience.

The most common media-linked responses that we found were classified as:

Objects of Prejudice, Disadvantaged, Poor Housing, Trouble, Numbers, Taking Job, Taking Houses and Anti-immigration.

These response categories are exemplified by statements like:

People are prejudiced against them, people discriminate against them, they are poor, they can't find jobs, they live in slums, they sleep ten to a room, they cause riots, there are too many of them coming in, there'll soon be more blacks than whites in this country, they take white people's jobs, they cause a housing shortage.

A few of these were also linked with personal experience in High areas for reasons we have discussed. Otherwise, the responses most characteristically derived from personal experience were:

Cultural Differences, Anti-stereotype, Favourable, Unfavourable, Equalitarian, Resentment, Culture Clash and Personal dislike.

Examples are:

Some are good, some are bad, just like whites; they are dirty; they are hardworking; they are clean; they should have the same rights as anyone else; their cooking stinks; they won't work but live on National Assistance; I can't stand them.

What the media-derived ideas have in common is that they are on the whole references to the general *state of affairs*, to what the situation in general is. Apart from Objects of Prejudice, none of the main media-linked responses is significantly related to attitude. The experience-derived responses on the other hand are almost all of an *affective/evaluative* nature.

In these experience-linked statements the expression of approval or disapproval, liking or disliking, outweighed any reference to the general state of affairs; the evaluative element was central.

Also consistent with this general pattern of results is that there is a much heavier evaluative emphasis in the parents' responses compared to the children's, together with the parents' much greater reference to personal experience as the source of their ideas . . .

It would appear that the media serve to define for people what the dimensions of the situation are. How they feel about the situation, thus defined, would seem to depend on other factors, particularly on where they live.

Hartmann and Husband, 1974

Questions

1 What are the main terms of reference in which the media covers the issue of race?
2 Would Hartmann and Husband's results suggest that prejudice is more likely to be higher in areas which have a large black population?
3 Given the general population's high rate of media consumption, to what extent is it valid to make a distinction between first hand knowledge and media-relayed knowledge?

Essay questions relating to Chapter 4

1 'The media's influence on its audience has been considerably exaggerated by its critics, be they conservative or radical.' Discuss.
2 Examine the extent to which the media constitute a major source of knowledge and beliefs in advanced industrial societies.

References

Becker, H. 1963. *The Outsiders*, Free Press, New York.

Berle, A. A. and Means, G. C. 1968. *The Modern Corporation and Private Property*, Harcourt Brace Jovanovich, New York.

Blumler, J., and Katz, E. (eds.) 1974. *The Uses of Mass Communication*, Sage Publications, Beverly Hills, California.

Burnham, J. 1960. *The Managerial Revolution*, Indiana University Press.

Burns, T. 1977. *The BBC: Public Institution and Private World*, Macmillan, London.

Cohen, S. 1972. *Folk Devils and Moral Panics*, MacGibbon and Kee, London.

Cohen, S., and Young, J. (eds.) 1972. *The Manufacture of News*, Constable, London.

Curran, J., Gurevitch, M., and Woollacott, J. (eds.) 1977. *Mass Communication and Society*, Edward Arnold, London.

Dominick, J., and Rauch, G. 1972. 'The image of women in network TV commercials', *Journal of Broadcasting*, No. 16, 1972, pp. 259–65.

Elliot, D. 1982. 'The Rock Music Industry in *Science, Technology and Popular Culture* (1), Open University Press, Milton Keynes.

Ellis, J. 1982. *Visible Fictions*, Routledge and Kegan Paul, London.

Eysenck, H. J. and Nias, D. K. 1978. *Sex, Violence and the Media*, Maurice Temple Smith, London.

Glasgow University Media Group 1976. *Bad News*, Routledge and Kegan Paul, London. *More Bad News*, 1980, Routledge and Kegan Paul, London.

Gurevitch, M., Bennett, T., Curran, J. and Woollacott, J. 1982. *Culture, Society and the Media*, Methuen, London.

Hall, S. *et al*. 1978. *Policing the Crisis*, Macmillan, London.

Halloran, J. P. 1970. *The Effects of Television*, Panther, St. Albans.

Harris, R. 1983. Gotcha! *The Media the Government and the Falklands Crisis*, Faber, London.

Harrison, M. 1985. *TV News: Whose Bias?* Policy Journals, London.

Hartmann, P., and Husband, C. 1974. *Racism and the Mass Media*, Davis Poynter, London.

Hood, S. 1980. *On Television*, Pluto, London.

Macshane, D. 1979. *Using the Media*, Pluto, London.

McQuail, D. (ed.) 1972. *Sociology of Mass Communication*, Penguin, London.

McQuail, D. 1983. *Mass Communication Theory: an Introduction*, Sage, Beverley Hills, California.

Marcuse, H. 1964. *One Dimensional Man*, Routledge and Kegan Paul, London.

Marx, K. 1965. *The German Ideology*, Lawrence and Wishart, London.

Morley, D. 1980. *The 'Nationwide' Audience*, British Film Institute, London.

Murdock, G., and Golding, P. *Capitalism, Communication and Class Relations* in Curran *et al.,* 1977.

Pearson, G. 1983. *Hooligan*, Macmillan, London.

Powdermaker, H. 1950. *Hollywood, The Dream Factory*, Little Bram, Boston.

Reith, J. 1949. *Into the Wind*, Hodder and Stoughton, London.

Tunstall, J. 1977. *The Media are American*, Constable, London.

Tunstall, J. 1983. *The Media in Britain*, Constable, London.

Waites, B., Bennett, T., and Martin, G. 1982. *Popular Culture: Past and Present*, Croom Helm, London.

For teachers wishing to extend their teaching of the media beyond A level Sociology into media studies the most useful source of publications is that of the British Film Institute – for a catalogue of their educational material, write to:
BFI Publications, 81 Dean Street, London W1V 6AA.

Further Reading

Berger, J. 1972. *Ways of Seeing*, Penguin, London.
A collection of essays on how we learn to read images.
Cohen, S., and Young, J. (eds.) 1972. *The Manufacture of News*, Constable, London.
A collection of readings on the media's treatment of various forms of deviance
Dyer, G. 1982. *Advertising as Communication*, Methuen, London.
A historical, economic, sociological and semiological examination of advertising.
Frith, S. 1983. *Sound Effects*, Constable, London.
A comprehensive sociological analysis of rock music.
Hartley, J. 1982. *Understanding News*, Methuen, London.
An account of how news is socially constructed and semiologically decoded.
Hobson, D. 1982. *'Crossroads', the Drama of a Soap Opera*, Methuen, London.
An insight into the making of TV soap opera, and its appeal to the audience.
Hood, S. 1980. *On Television*, Pluto, London.
An insider's critical view of television, but largely within a sociological framework.
Masterman, L. 1980. *Teaching about Television*, Macmillan, London.
A useful handbook for both teachers and students of television.
Tunstall, J. 1983. *The Media in Britain*, Constable, London.
A comprehensive factual summary of British media, and introduction to some of the key sociological debates.
Williams, R. 1974. *Television, Technology and Cultural Form*, Fontana, London.
A survey of the development of broadcasting in Britain and America, and an analysis of television forms and programme scheduling.

Index